Contents

LAW LIBRARY OF CONGRESS

BIOETHICS IN INTERNATIONAL LAW

Executive Summary

This report examines the field of bioethics from an international and regional legal perspective. It focuses on major international law documents such as the United Nations Universal Declaration on Bioethics and Human Rights and UNESCO declarations on human cloning and the human genome. Coverage of regional legal instruments includes the Council of Europe Convention on Human Rights and Biomedicine (the Oviedo Convention) and its Protocols on cloning, transplantation, and research with human beings. Work on surrogacy issues by the Hague Conference on Private International Law is also discussed, as are some African regional legal instruments on biosafety.

I. Introduction

Bioethics, as defined in article 1 of the Universal Declaration on Bioethics and Human Rights, concerns "ethical issues related to medicine, life sciences and associated technologies as applied to human beings, taking into account their social, legal and environmental dimensions."[1] It has been further characterized as an institutional tool for governance and policy making, as well as an influential field of academic research, which uses interdisciplinary methods and which covers within its scope "the analysis and development of norms for conduct and policy relating to the practice of medicine and healthcare, and the application of the life sciences and biomedicine to problems in medicine, health care, public health and health promotion."[2]

Because of the multidisciplinary aspects of bioethics, a number of international legal instruments have been adopted to deal with the various issues it covers. These documents have

---

[1] United Nations Educational, Scientific and Cultural Organization (UNESCO), The Universal Declaration on Bioethics and Human Rights (adopted on Oct. 19, 2005), http://www.unesco.org/new/en/social-and-human-sciences/themes/bioethics/bioethics-and-human-rights/. Ten years prior to the adoption of the Universal Declaration on Bioethics and Human Rights, in April 1995, the Inter-Parliamentary Union adopted a Resolution on Bioethics and Its Implications Worldwide for Human Rights Protection. For the text of the Resolution, *see* Bioethics and Its Implications Worldwide for Human Rights Protection, Resolution adopted by consensus by the 93rd Inter-Parliamentary Conference, Madrid (Apr. 1, 1995), http://www.ipu.org/conf-e/93-2 htm.

[2] Richard E. Ashcroft, *Could Human Rights Supersede Bioethics?* 10:4 HUMAN RIGHTS L. REV. 640–41 (2010), http://hrlr.oxfordjournals.org/content/10/4/639 full. Ashcroft notes that "[a]lthough there are long-standing debates about the status of bioethics as an actual or emergent academic discipline, given the protean nature of the field, and its complex interweaving into a wide range of institutional and professional settings, this identification of bioethics with its scope will be most helpful in understanding its main features." *Id.*

been formulated most notably by the United Nations (UNESCO in particular), but also by regional bodies such as the Council of Europe (COE) and the African Union. This report first examines international and regional legal instruments on bioethics in general and then turns to a consideration of specific aspects of the field treated under international and regional law. The report concludes with a brief look at possible future areas of international bioethics regulation.

II. Bioethics in General

A. The Universal Declaration on Bioethics and Human Rights

The Universal Declaration on Bioethics and Human Rights was adopted by acclamation at the 33rd General Conference of UNESCO on October 19, 2005. It takes note in its preamble not only of a number of major international civil and human rights instruments, but also of a long list of international and regional instruments in the field of bioethics. The latter include the Convention for the Protection of Human Rights and Dignity of the Human Being with regard to the Application of Biology and Medicine (the Convention on Human Rights and Biomedicine) and its additional protocols, national legislation and regulations in the field of bioethics, and the international and regional codes of conduct and guidelines and other texts in the field of bioethics. In addition, it recalls the Universal Declaration of Human Rights of December 10, 1948, the Universal Declaration on the Human Genome and Human Rights (adopted by the General Conference of UNESCO on November 11, 1997), and the International Declaration on Human Genetic Data (adopted by the General Conference of UNESCO on October 16, 2003).[3]

Among its stated aims, the Universal Declaration on Bioethics seeks "to provide a universal framework of principles and procedures to guide States in the formulation of their legislation, policies or other instruments in the field of bioethics"; "to promote respect for human dignity and protect human rights … consistent with international human rights law"; and "to recognize the importance of freedom of scientific research."[4] The principles include, for example, respect for human dignity and human rights; maximization of benefit and minimization of harm; respect for autonomy and individual responsibility; the necessity of carrying out medical intervention and scientific research only with the prior, free, and informed consent of the persons concerned; and respect for privacy and confidentiality.[5] The Declaration further provides for the establishment of independent ethics committees at the appropriate level to carry out such tasks as assessment of "the relevant ethical, legal, scientific and social issues related to research projects involving human beings," provision of advice on ethical problems in the clinical context, contribution to the preparation of guidelines on issues within the scope of the Declaration, and fostering of debate and public awareness of bioethics.[6]

---

[3] The Universal Declaration on Bioethics and Human Rights, *supra* note 1, preamble.

[4] *Id.* art. 2(a)–(d).

[5] *Id.* arts. 3–6, 9.

[6] *Id.* art. 19.

B. Convention on Human Rights and Biomedicine

The Council of Europe (COE) Convention for the Protection of Human Rights and Dignity of the Human Being with regard to the Application of Biology and Medicine, also known as the Oviedo Convention on Human Rights and Biomedicine, preceded the adoption of the Universal Declaration on Bioethics[7] and is "the first international treaty in this field."[8] The stated purpose of the Convention is for the Parties "to protect the dignity and identity of all human beings and guarantee everyone, without discrimination, respect for their integrity and other rights and fundamental freedoms with regard to the application of biology and medicine."[9] Other general concerns are the primacy of the human being "over the sole interest of society or science,"[10] provision of equitable access to health care,[11] and adherence to professional standards for "any intervention in the health field, including research."[12]

The Convention has a chapter on consent, with separate additional articles under other relevant chapters, to protect persons who are not able to give consent for scientific research or organ removal,[13] as well as chapters on the protection of private life and the right to information.[14] The Convention, unlike the Declaration, has discrete chapters on bioethical concerns involving the human genome, scientific research, and organ and tissue transplantation; on the prohibition of financial gain in regard to and provision for suitable disposal of the human body and its parts; and on acts constituting infringement of the Convention.[15]

---

[7] Convention for the Protection of Human Rights and Dignity of the Human Being with Regard to the Application of Biology and Medicine: Convention on Human Rights and Biomedicine (Oviedo, Apr. 4, 1997, in force on Dec. 1, 1999) (hereinafter COE Convention), ETS No. 164, http://conventions.coe.int/Treaty/en/Treaties/Html/164.htm.

[8] *Committee on Bioethics (DH-BIO)*, http://www.coe.int/t/dg3/healthbioethic/cdbi/default_en.asp (last visited Aug. 13, 2012). The Council of Europe, founded in 1949 and now comprising 49 member countries, "seeks to develop throughout Europe common and democratic principles based on the European Convention on Human Rights and other reference texts on the protection of individuals." *Who We Are*, http://www.coe.int/aboutCoe/index.asp?page=quisommesnous&l=en (last visited Aug. 15, 2012).

[9] COE Convention, *supra* note 7, art. 1.

[10] *Id.* art. 2.

[11] *Id.* art. 3.

[12] *Id.* art. 4.

[13] *Id.* ch. II.

[14] *Id.* ch. III.

[15] *Id.* chs. IV–VIII, respectively.

III. International and Regional Instruments on Specific Aspects of Bioethics

A. Cloning

The UN Declaration on Human Cloning, adopted in 2005,[16] recalls the Universal Declaration on the Human Genome and Human Rights of UNESCO "and in particular article 11 thereof, which states that practices which are contrary to human dignity, such as the reproductive cloning of human beings, shall not be permitted," and also UN Resolution 53/152 of December 9, 1998, endorsing the Universal Declaration on the Human Genome and Human Rights.[17] The General Assembly did not achieve consensus in the adoption of the human cloning declaration, however. Several delegations voted against the text because they contended that its reference to "human life" "could be interpreted as a call for a total ban on all forms of human cloning," while the United Kingdom representative saw it as a missed opportunity for adoption of a convention banning reproductive cloning, due to "the intransigence of those who were not prepared to recognize that other sovereign States might decide to permit strictly controlled applications of therapeutic cloning."[18]

In 1998, the COE Council of Ministers adopted a Protocol to the Oviedo Convention, on the prohibition of cloning human beings.[19] The Protocol clearly stipulates, in article 1, that "[a]ny intervention seeking to create a human being genetically identical to another human being, whether living or dead, is prohibited," defining the phrase "human being genetically

---

[16] United Nations Declaration on Human Cloning (adopted by the General Assembly on Mar. 8, 2005), http://www.wrtl.org/pdf/UN_onHumanCloning.pdf; *see also, e.g.*, Press Release, GA/10333, General Assembly Adopts United Nations Declaration on Human Cloning by Vote of 84-34-37 (Mar. 8, 2005), http://www.un.org/News/Press/docs/2005/ga10333.doc.htm; Nigel M. de S. Cameron & Anna V. Henderson, *Brave New World at the General Assembly: The United Nations Declaration on Human Cloning,* 9 MINN. J.L. SCI. & TECH. 145 (2008), *available at* Hein Online subscription database, http://heinonline.org/HOL/Page?handle=hein.journals/mipr9&div=7&collection=journals&set_as_cursor=1&men_t ab=srchresults&terms=35; George J. Annas, *The Changing Face of Family Law: Global Consequences of Embedding Physicians and Biotechnology in the Parent-Child Relationship*, 42 FAM. L.Q. 527–28 (2008–2009), Hein Online subscription database, http://heinonline.org/HOL/Page?handle=hein.journals/famlq42&div=33&collection=journals&set_as_cursor=0&me n_tab=srchresults&terms=35 (suggests the Declaration be followed by a formal treaty on The Preservation of the Human Species).

[17] United Nations Declaration on Human Cloning, *supra* note 16.

[18] Press Release, GA/10333, *supra* note 16.

[19] *Additional Protocol to the Convention for the Protection of Human Rights and Dignity of the Human Being with regard to the Application of Biology and Medicine, on the Prohibition of Cloning Human Beings (CETS No. 168) and Explanatory Report to the Protocol*, DIR/JUR (98) (opened for signature on Jan. 12, 1998, in force on Mar. 1, 2001), http://conventions.coe.int/Treaty/Commun/QueVoulezVous.asp?NT=168&CL=ENG; *see also* Henreitte D.C. Roscam Abbing, *A Council of Europe Protocol on Transplantation of Organs and Tissues of Human Origin*, 9 EUR. J. HEALTH L. 63 (2002), *available at* Hein Online subscription database, http://heinonline.org/HOL/Page?handle=hein.journals/eurjhlb9&div=13&collection=journals&set_as_cursor=0&me n_tab=srchresults&terms=A|Council|of|Europe|Protocol|on|Transplantation|of|Organs|and|Tissues|of|Human|Origin, &type=matchall.

identical to another human being" as "a human being sharing with another the same nuclear gene set."[20]

B. Human Genetics

The United Nations Convention on Biodiversity addresses, among other topics, access to genetic resources and the handling of biotechnology and distribution of its benefits.[21] The Convention, recognizing states' sovereign rights over their natural resources, stipulates that "the authority to determine access to genetic resources rests with the national governments and is subject to national legislation."[22] It also stipulates, among other provisions, that such access, when granted, will be on mutually agreed terms and will be subject to the prior informed consent of the Contracting Party providing those resources except as otherwise determined by that Party.[23] At the same time, Contracting Parties are to endeavor "to create conditions to facilitate access to genetic resources for sound uses by other Contracting Parties and not to impose restrictions counter to the Convention's objectives.[24]

UNESCO adopted the Universal Declaration on the Human Genome and Human Rights in 1997[25] and the International Declaration on Human Genetic Data in 2003.[26] The former contains sections on human dignity and the human genome, the rights of the persons concerned, research on the human genome, conditions for the exercise of scientific activity, and solidarity and international cooperation, among other topics. The International Declaration on Human Genetic Data covers, among other subjects, identity, the special status of human genetic data, and the purposes for which human genetic data and human proteomic data may be collected, processed, used, and stored as well as the procedures for conducting such activities. It also specifies the roles of UNESCO's International Bioethics Committee and Intergovernmental Bioethics Committee in implementing the Declaration.[27]

---

[20] Additional Protocol to the Convention for the Protection of Human Rights and Dignity of the Human Being with regard to the Application of Biology and Medicine, on the Prohibition of Cloning Human Beings (Jan. 12, 1998), art. 1, http://conventions.coe.int/Treaty/en/Treaties/Html/168.htm.

[21] Convention on Biological Diversity (June 5, 1992), http://treaties.un.org/doc/Treaties/1992/06/1992 0605%2008-44%20PM/Ch_XXVII_08p.pdf; *The Convention on Biodiversity*, http://www.cbd.int/convention/ (last visited Aug. 15, 2012) (click on hyperlink in left-hand column for the text of the Convention).

[22] *Id.* art. 15(1).

[23] *Id.* art. 15(4) & (5).

[24] *Id.* art. 15(2).

[25] Universal Declaration on the Human Genome and Human Rights (adopted by UNESCO's 29th General Conference on Nov. 11, 1997, and endorsed by the 53rd Session of the UN General Assembly by Resolution A/RES/53/152 on Dec. 9, 1998), http://www.unesco.org/new/en/social-and-human-sciences/themes/bioethics/human-genome-and-human-rights/.

[26] International Declaration on Human Genetic Data (adopted by UNESCO's 32nd General Conference on Oct. 16, 2003), http://www.unesco.org/new/en/social-and-human-sciences/themes/bioethics/human-genetic-data/.

[27] *Id.* art. 25.

Another Protocol to the Oviedo Convention, on genetic testing for health purposes, has not yet entered into force.[28]

C. Biosafety and Genetically Modified Organisms

Various international instruments address biosafety and in particular the ethical aspects of the international movement of living modified organisms (LMOs) resulting from biotechnology. Three such instruments are the Cartagena Protocol on Biosafety to the Convention on Biodiversity,[29] its supplementary protocol on liability and redress,[30] and the Nagoya Protocol on Access to Genetic Resources and the Fair and Equitable Sharing of Benefits Arising from Their Utilization to the Convention on Biological Diversity.[31] The Cartagena Protocol applies "to the transboundary movement, transit, handling and use of all living modified organisms that may have adverse effects on the conservation and sustainable use of biological diversity, taking also into account risks to human health," but not to the transboundary movement of LMOs "which are pharmaceuticals for humans that are addressed by other relevant international agreements or organisations."[32] An international standard pertaining to living modified organisms is the Risk Analysis Principles for Foods Derived from Biotechnology of the UN Codex Alimentarius Commission.[33]

---

[28] Additional Protocol to the Convention on Human Rights and Biomedicine Concerning Genetic Testing for Health Purposes, CETS No. 203 (opened for signature on Nov. 27, 2008), http://conventions.coe.int/ Treaty/Commun/QueVoulezVous.asp?NT=203&CM=1&CL=ENG. Five ratifications including four COE Member States are required in order for the Protocol to enter into force; thus far only Moldova and Slovenia (both Member States) have ratified the Protocol. *Status as of: 13/8/2012*, http://conventions.coe.int/Treaty/Commun/ ChercheSig.asp?NT=203&CM=1&DF=&CL=ENG (last visited Aug. 13, 2012). One lengthy study of the subject of bioethics and biosafety is M.K. SATEESH, BIOETHICS AND BIOSAFETY (I.K. Inter'l Pvt. Ltd., 2008).

[29] Cartagena Protocol on Biosafety to the Convention on Biodiversity (adopted on Jan. 29, 2000, and in force on Sept. 11, 2003), http://bch.cbd.int/protocol/ (hyperlink to the Protocol text is in left-hand column), certified true copy *available at* http://treaties.un.org/doc/Treaties/2000/01/20000129%2008- 44%20PM/Ch_XXVII_08_ap.pdf.

[30] Nagoya – Kuala Lumpur Supplementary Protocol on Liability and Redress to the Cartagena Protocol on Biosafety (closed for signature after Mar. 6, 2012), http://bch.cbd.int/protocol/supplementary/ (has link to text in left-hand column), certified true copy *available at* http://treaties.un.org/doc/source/signature/2011/Ch-XXVII-8- c.pdf.

[31] The Nagoya – Kuala Lumpur Supplementary Protocol on Liability and Redress to the Cartagena Protocol on Biosafety (adopted on Oct. 29, 2010, and opened for signature from Feb. 2, 2011, until Feb. 1, 2012), http://bch.cbd.int/protocol/supplementary/ (last updated June 26, 2012), certified true copy *available at* http://treaties.un.org/doc/source/signature/2010/Ch-XXVII-8-b-Corr-Original.pdf.

[32] Cartagena Protocol on Biosafety to the Convention on Biodiversity, *supra* note 29, arts. 4 & 5.

[33] Risk Analysis Principles for Foods Derived from Biotechnology, CAC/GL 44-2003 (adopted in 2003, as amended in 2008 & 2011), http://www.codexalimentarius.org/standards/list-of-standards/en/ (scroll down page to the title and click on green check mark for English version); The Codex Alimentarius Commission (CAC) "is an intergovernmental body with more than 180 members, within the framework of the Joint Food Standards Programme established by the Food and Agriculture Organization of the United Nations (FAO) and the World Health Organization (WHO)." CODEX ALIMENTARIUS: FOODS DERIVED FROM MODERN BIOTECHNOLOGY (2d ed. 2009), ftp://ftp.fao.org/docrep/fao/011/a1554e/a1554e00.pdf.

The intergovernmental African Union (AU), which succeeded the Organization of African Unity (OAU) in 2002 and now comprises fifty-four member states,[34] has initiatives on biosafety that include the establishment of the High Level Panel on Biotechnology, the formulation of an African position on GMOs, and the drafting of an African Model Law on Biosafety.[35] The AU's draft Revised African Model Law on Biosafety was finalized in May 2001,[36] and the latest draft text appears to date from 2008.[37] According to one African agricultural official, "[t]he law proceeds on the assumption that measures provided for in the Cartagena Protocol on Bio-safety are minimum, hence African States on the basis of their sovereign rights could adopt more rigorous standards on the subject," and so the Model Law "sets out additional bio-safety measures that are not dealt with in the Cartagena Protocol on Bio-safety i.e. labelling and redress as well as LMOs for food, feed and processing among others."[38]

In addition, subregions, or regional economic communities (RECs), of Africa have also undertaken initiatives related to biosafety. The South African Development Community was the first REC to develop guidelines on issues of GMOs and biotechnology.[39] The Common Market for Eastern and Southern Africa (COMESA) has undertaken the "Regional Approach to Biotechnology and Biosafety Policy in Eastern and Southern Africa" (RABESA) project in order to harmonize the biosafety policies of its Member States.[40] According to a 2010 news report, the Economic Community of West African States (ECOWAS) was "developing a common biosafety regulation in line with the national biosafety laws and regulations in the sub-region."[41]

---

[34] *Profile: African Union*, BBC NEWS (Feb. 1, 2012), http://news.bbc.co.uk/2/hi/africa/country_profiles/3870303.stm.

[35] Sarah A. H. Olembo, *An African Position on GMOs in Agriculture and Food Security*, 12th ICARB Conference, Ravello (2008), slide no. 22, http://www.economia.uniroma2.it/icabr/Public//File/Olembo.pdf (PowerPoint presentation).

[36] *African Model Law on Biosafety*, http://www.africa-union.org/root/au/auc/departments/hrst/biosafety/AU_Biosafety_2b htm (last visited Aug. 14, 2012).

[37] Revised African Model Law on Biosafety (Draft) (Jan. 2008), http://www.africa-union.org/root/au/auc/departments/hrst/biosafety/DOC/level2/DraftRevAMLBS_Jan08_EN.pdf.

[38] Olembo, *supra* note 35, slide no. 27.

[39] *Id.*, slide no. 29.

[40] David Wafula et al., *The RABESA Project 2004-2011: Achievements and Future Prospects* (Nov. 2011), http://www.asareca.org/sites/default/files/Status%20of%20RABESA%20updated.pdf; *see also Biotech Experts Convene to Develop Regional GM Policy for Eastern and Southern Africa*, CROP BIOTECH UPDATE (May 18, 2012), http://www.isaaa.org/kc/cropbiotechupdate/newsletter/default.asp?Date=5/18/2012#9602.

[41] *ECOWAS Plans Common Regional Biosafety Regulation, Nigeria Adopted Biosafety Bill* (Aug. 24, 2010), http://www.gmo-free-regions.org/de/gmo-free-regions/albania/gmo-free-news-from-albania/news/en/22431.html. Work on this project appears to be ongoing; according to a March 2011 news item, ECOWAS was formulating a Common Regulatory Framework on a Draft Protocol on Biosafety/Biotechnology. *Workshop on ECOWAS Protocol on Biosafety*, GOVERNMENT OF GHANA OFFICIAL PORTAL (Mar. 16, 2011), http://www.ghana.gov.gh/index.php/news/general-news/5149-workshop-on-ecowas-protocol-on-biosafety.

D. Transplantation

The Additional Protocol to the Oviedo Convention concerning human organ and tissue transplantation entered in force in May 2006.[42] The Protocol's purpose "is to define and safeguard the rights of organ and tissue donors, whether living or deceased, and those of persons receiving implants of organs and tissues of human origin."[43] The Protocol applies to transplants of organs, tissues, and cells of human origin only, carried out for therapeutic purposes. It expressly does not apply to reproductive organs and tissue; embryonic or fetal organs and tissues; or blood and blood derivatives.[44] "Transplantation" is defined in the Protocol as "the complete process of removal of an organ or tissue from one person and implantation of that organ or tissue into another person, including all procedures for preparation, preservation and storage."[45] The Protocol covers organ and tissue removal from living persons,[46] from deceased persons,[47] and from a person undergoing medical procedures for their own benefit, for a purpose other than donation for an implantation, who may consent to implantation of their removed organ or tissue.[48] The Protocol expressly prohibits financial gain arising from the human body and its parts[49] as well as organ trafficking.[50]

E. Research with Human Beings

Another specific field of bioethics in which efforts have been made to adopt universal guidelines is the field of research with human beings. The Additional Protocol to the Oviedo Convention concerning biomedical research, which came into force in September 2007, "covers the full range of research activities in the health field involving interventions on human beings."[51] It applies to research on fetuses and embryos *in vivo*, but not *in vitro*.[52] Intervention

---

[42] Additional Protocol to the Convention on Human Rights and Biomedicine Concerning Transplantation of Organs and Tissues of Human Origin, CETS No. 186 (opened for signature on Jan. 24, 2002, in force on May 1, 2006), http://conventions.coe.int/Treaty/Commun/QueVoulezVous.asp?NT=186&CL=ENG. *See also*, *e.g.*, Abbing, *supra* note 19.

[43] Explanatory Report: Additional Protocol to the Convention on Human Rights and Biomedicine Concerning Transplantation of Organs and Tissues of Human Origin, http://conventions.coe.int/Treaty/ en/Reports/Html/186 htm (last visited Aug. 16, 2012).

[44] Additional Protocol to the Convention on Human Rights and Biomedicine Concerning Transplantation of Organs and Tissues of Human Origin, *supra* note 42, art. 2(3).

[45] *Id.* art. 2(4).

[46] *Id.* ch. III, arts. 9–15.

[47] *Id.* ch. IV, arts. 16–19.

[48] *Id.* ch. V, art. 20.

[49] *Id.* art. 21.

[50] *Id.* art. 22.

[51] Additional Protocol to the Convention on Human Rights and Biomedicine, Concerning Biomedical Research, CETS No. 195 (opened for signature on Jan. 25, 2005, in force on Sept. 1, 2007), art. 2(1), http://conventions.coe.int/Treaty/Commun/QueVoulezVous.asp?NT=195&CL=ENG (click on hyperlink to HTML or PDF text).

[52] *Id.* art. 2(2).

is defined under the Protocol as including a physical intervention as well as "any other intervention in so far as it involves a risk to the psychological health of the person concerned."[53] The document asserts the primacy of the human being, stating that "the interests and welfare of the human being participating in research shall prevail over the sole interest of society or science."[54] While research is to be carried out freely, subject to the Protocol's provisions and other relevant legal provisions ensuring the protection of the human being,[55] it "may only be undertaken if there is no alternative of comparable effectiveness."[56]

F. Surrogacy

At present there is no dedicated international agreement on surrogacy, but efforts are underway that might evolve into the formulation of such an instrument. The Hague Conference on International Private Law (HCCH) announced on April 7, 2011, that issues of cross-frontier surrogacy had been added to its work program. The mandate of the Permanent Bureau, the Secretariat of the HCCH, is "to gather information on the practical legal needs in the area, comparative developments in domestic and private international law, and the prospects of achieving consensus on a global approach to addressing international surrogacy issues."[57] The Permanent Bureau also presented a preliminary report on the subject in April 2011 to a meeting of the Council on General Affairs and Policy of the HCCH.[58] A few months after this development, the Nuffield Foundation, a charitable trust that works mostly in the United Kingdom, awarded a grant for a two-year study on the private international law aspects of international surrogacy agreements, commencing on August 1, 2010.[59]

IV. Future Steps

As noted above (under "Human Genetics"), a Protocol to the Oviedo Convention on genetic testing for health purposes has been opened for signature but is not yet in force. Steps are also being taken that might result in the adoption of an international legal instrument on

---

[53] *Id.* art. 2(3).

[54] *Id.* art. 3.

[55] *Id.* art. 4.

[56] *Id.* art. 5.

[57] Press Release, Hague Conference on Private International Law, Cross-Frontier Surrogacy Issues Added to Hague Conference Work Programme (Apr. 7, 2011), http://www.hcch.net/index_en.php?act=events.details&year=2011&varevent=216.

[58] Permanent Bureau, Private International Law Issues Surrounding the Status of Children, Including Issues Arising from International Surrogacy Arrangements, Preliminary Document No. 11 (Mar. 2011), http://www.hcch net/upload/wop/genaff2011pd11e.pdf.

[59] *International Surrogacy Arrangements: An Urgent Need for a Legal Regulation at the International Level*, http://www.abdn.ac.uk/law/surrogacy/; Martin George, *A Study on the Private International Law Aspects of International Surrogacy Agreements* (Sept. 21, 2010), http://conflictoflaws net/2010/a-study-on-the-private-international-law-aspects-of-international-surrogacy-agreements/. *See also* Kristiana Brugger, *International Law in the Gestational Surrogacy Debate*, 35 FORDHAM INT'L L.J. 685 (2011–2012), HeinOnline subscription database, http://heinonline.org/HOL/Page?handle=hein.journals/frdint35&div=22&collection=journals&set_as_cursor=15&men_tab=srchresults&terms=6.

surrogacy. A Nuffield Council on Bioethics study on donor conception was begun in February 2012, to be completed this year.[60]

Other areas affecting bioethics in which international legal action may be taken are the protection of the human embryo in vitro, a topic on which the COE produced a report in 2003[61] and xenotransplantation ("transplantation of organs originating from animals").[62] In addition, nongovernmental studies are being undertaken on the ethics of novel neurotechnologies (intervention in the brain)[63] and emerging biotechnologies (e.g., synthetic biology and nanotechnology).[64]

Prepared by Wendy Zeldin
Senior Legal Research Analyst
September 2012

---

[60] *Donor Conception: Ethical Aspects of Information Disclosure*, NUFFIELD COUNCIL ON BIOETHICS, http://www.nuffieldbioethics.org/donor-conception (last visited Aug. 16, 2012).

[61] Steering Committee on Bioethics, *The Protection of the Human Embryo In Vitro*, Report by the Working Party on the Protection of the Human Embryo and Fetus (CDBI-CO-GT3) (June 19, 2003), http://www.coe.int/t/dg3/healthbioethic/activities/04_human_embryo_and_foetus_en/CDBI-CO-GT3(2003)13E.pdf.

[62] *Xenotransplantation*, http://www.coe.int/t/dg3/healthbioethic/Activities/06_Xenotransplantation_en/default_en.asp (last visited Aug. 16, 2012). A Working Party on the subject was established under the (then) Steering Committee on Bioethics; it finalized draft guidelines on xenotransplantation that were approved by the Steering Committee and the European Health Committee in June 2002 and adopted in a COE Council of Ministers Recommendation on June 19, 2003. For the text of the Recommendation, which includes the Guidelines, *see* Recommendation Rec(2003)10 of the Committee of Ministers to Member States on Xenotransplantation (June 19, 2003), https://wcd.coe.int/ViewDoc.jsp?id=45827.

[63] *Novel Technologies: Intervening in the Brain*, NUFFIELD COUNCIL ON BIOETHICS, http://www.nuffieldbioethics.org/neurotechnology (last visited Aug. 16, 2012).

[64] *Emerging Biotechnologies: Ethical Issues*, NUFFIELD COUNCIL ON BIOETHICS, http://www.nuffieldbioethics.org/emerging-biotechnologies (last visited Aug. 16, 2012). The Nuffield study is due to be ready in the fall of 2012. *See also Special Issue: Human Rights and New Technologies*, 10:4 HUMAN RIGHTS L. REV. (Dec. 2010), http://hrlr.oxfordjournals.org/content/10/4.toc.

LAW LIBRARY OF CONGRESS

UNITED KINGDOM

STEM CELL RESEARCH AND HUMAN EMBRYOS

Executive Summary

The United Kingdom has emerged as an international leader in the field of stem cell research, through a system of relatively permissive regulation and grants to encourage development. It permits the use and creation of embryos for research purposes, with a system of licensing and oversight provided by the Human Fertilisation and Embryology Authority.

I. Introduction

The United Kingdom seeks to be an international leader in the field of stem cell research, actively encouraging development through a relatively liberal legislative regime and a system of government grants.[1] It has established the UK Stem Cell Initiative, which aims to make the UK "the most scientifically and commercially productive location for this activity."[2]

The term stem cell is defined in a popular medical dictionary as "[a]n unspecialized cell found in fetuses, embryos, and some adult body tissues that has the potential to develop into specialized cells or divide into other stem cells."[3] A Select Committee of the House of Lords describes stem cells as having:

> the capacity to undergo an asymmetric division such that one of the two "daughter" cells retains the properties of the stem cell while the other begins to "differentiate" into a more specialised cell type. . . . Stem cells are thus central to normal human growth and development, and are also a potential source of new cells for the regeneration of diseased or damaged tissue.[4]

There are four main sources of stem cells: embryo, fetus, cord blood and adult.[5] While these sources all have the potential to renew tissue, embryonic stem cells offer the most

---

[1] MEDICAL RESEARCH COUNCIL, STEM CELLS: STEM CELL SCIENCE IN THE UK (2008), http://www.hta.gov.uk/_db/_documents/stem_cell_pack_200806170144.pdf.

[2] *UK Stem Cell Initiative (UKSCI)*, DEPARTMENT OF HEALTH, http://www.dh.gov.uk/ab/UKSCI/DH_098510 (last visited Aug. 6, 2012).

[3] AMERICAN HERITAGE SCIENCE DICTIONARY (2010), *available at* http://science.yourdictionary.com/stem-cell (last visited Aug. 15, 2012).

[4] SELECT COMMITTEE ON STEM CELL RESEARCH, REPORT, 2002, H.L. 83(i), ¶ 2.2, *available at* http://www.parliament.the-stationery-office.co.uk/pa/ld200102/ldselect/ldstem/83/8301.htm (last visited Aug. 6, 2012).

[5] SELECT COMMITTEE ON STEM CELL RESEARCH, REPORT vol. 2, 2002, H.L. 83(ii), at 470.

promising therapeutic potential, as they are pluripotent and therefore "retain the ability to develop into nearly any cell type of the body."[6]

The use of embryonic stem cells for research raises a number of ethical issues over the use and resulting destruction of embryos for research purposes. This report addresses the legislative framework regulating the use of human embryos and the issues the British government considered when deciding to permit the use of human embryos for research purposes.

II. Status of the Embryo In Research

After the birth of the first baby created through the in vitro fertilization (IVF) process in 1978, the government established the Committee of Inquiry into Human Fertilisation and Embryology, also known as the Warnock Committee, to review the ethical and social issues surrounding the use of human embryos in research and IVF treatment.[7] One mandate of the Warnock Committee was to recommend legislation regulating the use of these embryos.[8] The committee heard evidence from various scientific, religious, and ethical bodies on the moral and legal status of the human embryo. It recommended that while "the human embryo is entitled to a measure of respect beyond that accorded to an embryo of other species, . . . [s]uch respect is not absolute and may be weighed against the benefits arising from proposed research."[9] The committee determined that research on human embryos is morally justified in certain circumstances, and made a number of recommendations.[10] These recommendations led to the enactment of the Human Fertilisation and Embryology Act 1990,[11] the first piece of legislation in the United Kingdom to regulate scientific research on human embryos.

---

[6] DEPARTMENT OF HEALTH, CHIEF MEDICAL OFFICER'S EXPERT GROUP REPORT, STEM CELL RESEARCH: MEDICAL PROGRESS WITH RESPONSIBILITY, June 2000, ¶¶ 1.6 & 2.18, *available at* http://www.dh.gov.uk/assetRoot/04/06/50/85/04065085.pdf. (last visited Aug. 8, 2012).

[7] The terms of reference of the Warnock Committee were to "consider recent and potential developments in medicine and sciences related to human fertilization and embryology; to consider what policies and safeguards should be applied, including consideration of the social, ethical and legal implications of these developments; and to make recommendations." DEPARTMENT OF HEALTH & SOCIAL SECURITY, REPORT OF THE COMMITTEE OF INQUIRY INTO HUMAN FERTILISATION AND EMBRYOLOGY, 1984, Cmnd. 9314, *quoted in* ALEX SLEATOR, HOUSE OF COMMONS LIBRARY, RESEARCH PAPER 00/93, STEM CELL RESEARCH AND REGULATIONS UNDER THE *HUMAN FERTILISATION AND EMBRYOLOGY ACT 1990* 14 (Revised Edition Dec. 13, 2000), *available at* http://www.parliament.uk/briefing-papers/RP00-93.

[8] *Id.*

[9] DEPARTMENT OF HEALTH, *supra* note 6, ¶ 4.6, Box 17.

[10] The government issued a consultation paper and a white paper detailing the government's policy prior to enacting the 1990 Act: LEGISLATION ON HUMAN INFERTILITY SERVICES AND EMBRYO RESEARCH, 1986, Cm 46; DEPARTMENT OF HEALTH AND SOCIAL SECURITY, HUMAN FERTILISATION AND EMBRYOLOGY: A FRAMEWORK FOR LEGISLATION, 1987, Cm. 259.

[11] Human Fertilisation and Embryology Act 1990, c. 37, http://www.legislation.gov.uk/ukpga/1990/37/contents. This legislation has substantially been amended by the Human Fertilisation and Embryology Act 2008, c. 22, http://www.legislation.gov.uk/ukpga/2008/22/contents, to reflect developments in technology and attitudes towards the use of embryos in research.

After the decision to allow research on embryos, the government next considered the ethically acceptable period in which embryos should be used in research. As a result of a recommendation from the Warnock Committee, the Human Fertilisation and Embryology Act granted the Human Fertilisation and Embryology Authority (HFEA) the authority to issue licenses for research on embryos up to fourteen days old, or when the primitive streak[12] appears, whichever occurs first.[13]

III. The Human Fertilisation and Embryology Act 1990

The Human Fertilisation and Embryology Act prohibits the creation, use, or storage of a human embryo or gametes[14] without a license issued by the HFEA,[15] a regulatory body established by the Act. If a person creates a human embryo without a license from the HFEA, they are guilty of an offense and are liable, upon indictment, to imprisonment for up to two years and/or a fine.[16]

The HFEA is accountable to Parliament and ensures through a system of licensing that human embryos are used only for the purposes specified in the Act. The Human Fertilisation and Embryology Act limits the use of human embryos in research by specifying the purposes for which the HFEA can issue a license. These purposes are:

(a) increasing knowledge about serious disease or other serious medical conditions,

(b) developing treatments for serious disease or other serious medical conditions,

(c) increasing knowledge about the causes of any congenital disease or congenital medical condition that does not fall within paragraph (a),

(d) promoting advances in the treatment of infertility,

(e) increasing knowledge about the causes of miscarriage,

(f) developing more effective techniques of contraception,

(g) developing methods for detecting the presence of gene, chromosome or mitochondrion abnormalities in embryos before implantation, or

(h) increasing knowledge about the development of embryos.[17]

The HFEA has discretion to ensure that embryos are not arbitrarily used in research. Not only must a license applicant meet one of the above purposes, but the HFEA also must be satisfied that the use of the embryo is necessary or desirable for that purpose.[18] Once a license

---

[12] The primitive streak is defined as "[a] collection of cells from which the human central nervous system eventually develops." SELECT COMMITTEE ON STEM CELL RESEARCH, *supra* note 4, ¶ 1.3 n.3.

[13] Human Fertilisation ad Embryology Act 1990, c. 37, §§ 3(3)(a), 3(4). The 14 day period does not apply to any time that the embryo is kept in storage. DEPARTMENT OF HEALTH, *supra* note 6, ¶ 3.8.

[14] Human Fertilisation and Embryology Act 1990, c. 37, §§ 3, 4.

[15] HUMAN FERTILISATION AND EMBRYOLOGY AUTHORITY, http://www.hfea.gov.uk/ (last visited Aug. 8, 2012).

[16] Human Fertilisation and Embryology Act 1990, c. 37, § 41.

[17] Human Fertilisation and Embryology Act 1990, c. 37, sched. 2, ¶ 3A(2), *amended by* Human Fertilisation and Embryology Act 2008, c. 22, sched. 2, ¶ 6.

[18] Human Fertilisation and Embryology Act 1990, c. 37, sched. 2, ¶ 3A(1), *amended by* Human Fertilisation and Embryology Act 2008, c. 22, sched. 2, ¶ 6.

has been granted, the HFEA maintains continued oversight of research projects; licensees must provide reports to the HFEA every six to twelve months and produce a final report at the end of the project detailing all results and conclusions.[19]

To ensure that the act maintains pace with scientific and technological developments, it includes a provision that allows the scope of research for which licenses can be granted to be expanded through secondary legislation.[20] It is unusual to allow the expansion of the scope of primary legislation through secondary legislation. In this case, to ensure that secondary legislation on such a contentious issue cannot quietly be passed without debate, a draft must be placed before both the House of Lords and House of Commons and approved by a resolution in each House.[21]

IV. Embryos and Stem Cell Research

After considerable debate in Parliament and a number of government and department reports[22] regarding the moral, ethical, and public policy implications of research on human embryos, the government determined that the purposes for which research on embryos could be undertaken should be extended to allow stem cell research. The government concluded that this could occur without unjustifiably extending the use of embryos under the Human Fertilisation and Embryology Act.[23]

In legalizing the use of embryos for the purposes of research, various government reports rejected the argument that equivalent research could be conducted solely with adult stem cells. The government was "satisfied on the basis of the scientific evidence that as yet research on

---

[19] Human Fertilisation and Embryology Act 1990, c. 37, § 12(1)(g). HUMAN FERTILISATION AND EMBRYOLOGY AUTHORITY, TWENTY FIRST ANNUAL REPORT AND ACCOUNTS 2010/11, 2011, at 15, *available at* http://www.hfea.gov.uk/docs/ISBN_978-0-10-297633-5_WEB.pdf.

[20] Human Fertilisation and Embryology Act 1990, c. 37, § 45(4). This section permits the Secretary of State to enact regulations via statutory instrument. This section further provides that if a statutory instrument containing regulations that has not been approved in draft form by a resolution of each House of Parliament, it is subject to annulment by a resolution of either House.

[21] *See generally* ERSKINE MAY, ERSKINE MAY'S TREATISE ON THE LAW, PRIVILEGES, PROCEEDINGS AND USAGE OF PARLIAMENT (Sir. William McKay et al. eds., 23rd ed. 2004), 666-701; *see also* JOINT COMMITTEE ON DELEGATED LEGISLATION, SECOND REPORT, 1972-2, H.L. 204, H.C. 468, ¶ 49, in which the government agreed to avoid using the positive resolution procedure under normal circumstances.

[22] DEPARTMENT OF HEALTH, DEPARTMENT OF TRADE AND INDUSTRY & OFFICE OF SCIENCE AND TECHNOLOGY: CLONING ISSUES IN REPRODUCTION, SCIENCE AND MEDICINE, 1999, Cm. 4387; DEPARTMENT OF HEALTH, STEM CELL RESEARCH: MEDICAL PROGRESS WITH RESPONSIBILITY, 2000, Cm. 4833, *available at* http://www.dh.gov.uk/prod_consum_dh/groups/dh_digitalassets/@dh/@en/documents/digitalasset/dh_4065085.pdf; HUMAN GENETICS ADVISORY COMMISSION & HUMAN FERTILISATION AND EMBRYOLOGY AUTHORITY, CLONING ISSUES IN REPRODUCTION, SCIENCE AND MEDICINE, 1998, *available at* http://www.hfea.gov.uk/docs/Cloning_Issue_Report.pdf.

[23] DEPARTMENT OF HEALTH, *supra* note 6, ¶ 4.3. This move was initially provided for through the Human Fertilisation and Embryology (Research Purposes) Regulations 2001, SI 2001/188, which added additional purposes for which the HFEA could issue a license. This regulation has since been revoked by the Human Fertilisation and Embryology Act 2008, c. 22, http://www.legislation.gov.uk/ukpga/2008/22/contents, which made provision for these purposes.

adult stem cells has not, as some claim, made research on embryonic stem cells unnecessary."[24] Successive government and scientific reports examining the issue echoed the reasoning of the Warnock Committee in 1978, concluding:

> the great potential to relieve suffering and treat disease mean[s] that research [is] warranted across the whole range of possible sources of stem cells . . . including embryos. . . . [T]he potential benefit of discovering the mechanism for reprogramming adult cells and thereby providing compatible tissue for treatment justifies this transitional research involving the creation of embryos by cell nuclear replacement [CNR].[25]

The House of Lords Select Committee on Stem Cell Research, appointed to examine the scientific, ethical, social and religious issues surrounding the regulations,[26] agreed with the view that the embryo has a special status as a potential human being that increases as the embryo develops. However, it concluded that the respect due to the embryo in the early stages should be weighed against the potential benefits arising from the proposed research, and after "having weighed the ethical arguments carefully, . . . was not persuaded . . . that all research on early human embryos should be prohibited."[27]

V. Creation of Embryos for Research

The Human Fertilisation and Embryology Act permitted the creation of embryos specifically for research.[28] It is believed that stem cells derived from embryos created by CNR are therapeutically valuable as they are "genetically compatible with the person being treated, from whom the donor nucleus [originates]."[29] The creation of stem cells using CNR is also known as "therapeutic cloning."

---

[24] Roger Highfield, *Lords Back Research on Cloned Embryo Stem Cells*, DAILY TELEGRAPH (London) Feb. 28, 2002, at 11 (quoting Rt. Rev. Richard Harries, Chairman, House of Lords Select Comm. on Stem Cell Research).

[25] DEPARTMENT OF HEALTH, *supra* note 6, ¶¶ 25 and 28. The Expert Group lists the benefits of research involving CNR as: "understanding how adult cells can be reprogrammed; establishing the role of the egg in reprogramming an adult nucleus; discovering whether stem cells derived from embryos created by CNR differentiate in the same way and have the same potential as stem cells derived from embryos created from eggs and sperm; clarifying whether the stem cells from embryos created by CNR can produce tissue compatible with the donor of the nucleus; [and] clarifying whether concepts developed in animal studies apply to humans, in particular the conditions required to achieve CNR in a human egg." *Id.* at 31.

[26] The idea for a Select Committee was put forward in the House of Lords during debates on the draft regulations. A peer of the House of Lords advocated that the regulations should be rejected until a Select Committee reviewed the issues, but this view was not followed, and a Select Committee was appointed retrospectively to review the issues surrounding the regulations. *See* 621 PARL. DEB., H.L. (5th ser.) (2001) 15, *available at*: http://www.parliament.the-stationery-office.co.uk/pa/ld200001/ldhansrd/vo010122/text/10122-04.htm#10122-04_head2 (last visited Aug. 8, 2012).

[27] HOUSE OF LORDS, *supra* note 4, ¶ 4.21.

[28] Embryos are created either through IVF or CNR, which is the process where "an embryo is created by the replacement of the nucleus of an unfertilized egg by the nucleus of another cell." DEPARTMENT OF HEALTH, *supra* note 6, at 24. Between the years 1991-1998 763,509 embryos were created by IVF, predominantly for infertility treatment. Out of that figure, 48,444 were given for use in research, 118 were created in the course of research and 237,603 were not used for any purpose and destroyed. *Id.* ¶ 3.5.

[29] DEPARTMENT OF HEALTH, *supra* note 6, ¶ 2.28.

Because of the sensitivity of the issues raised, the House of Lords Select Committee on Stem Cell Research took up consideration of this question. After examining the evidence, it reiterated the view of the Warnock Committee[30] and ratified the policy followed by the HFEA that "embryos should not be created specifically for research purposes unless there is a demonstrable and exceptional need which cannot be met by the use of surplus embryos."[31]

While there is no distinction in the 1990 Act between embryos created through CNR or fertilization, the government determined that HFEA was the appropriate body to deal with ethical concerns over the use of embryos created by CNR, as it grants licenses on a case-by-case basis, and must follow statutory criteria.[32] The HFEA granted the first license for the use of therapeutic cloning in research in August 2004.[33]

Prepared by Clare Feikert-Ahalt
Senior Foreign Law Specialist
August 2012

---

[30] The Warnock Committee recommended by a narrow margin that embryos could be created solely for research. At the time, the Committee considered this situation unlikely to arise as most needs could be met with embryos created for IVF treatment that are either not suitable for use or later not needed. HUMAN FERTILISATION AND EMBRYOLOGY AUTHORITY, NINTH ANNUAL REPORT AND ACCOUNTS, 2000, *cited in* HOUSE OF LORDS, *supra* note 4.

[31] HOUSE OF LORDS, *supra* note 4, ¶ 6.

[32] DEPARTMENT OF HEALTH, *supra* note 6, ¶ 13.

[33] *HFEA Grants the First Therapeutic Cloning Licence for Research*, HUMAN FERTILISATION AND EMBRYOLOGY AUTHORITY, August 11, 2004, http://www.hfea.gov.uk/758.html.

LAW LIBRARY OF CONGRESS

GERMANY

RESTRICTIONS ON EMBRYONIC STEM CELL RESEARCH

Executive Summary

Germany permits embryonic stem cell research only if carried out on imported stem cell lines derived from embryos that were created before May 1, 2007, for reproductive purposes. Stem cell research in violation of these restrictions is a criminal offense. Although the regime appears very restrictive, it nevertheless allows for the importation of enough stem cell lines to give German researchers the opportunity to engage in basic and clinical research.

The complexity of the German rules reflects the ongoing tension between ethical values on the one hand and scientific interests on the other. Whereas the constitutional guarantees of human dignity and the right to life may apply to the embryo, the Constitution also guarantees the freedom of science. Whereas the Embryo Protection Act prohibits the use of embryos for any purposes other than bringing about a pregnancy, the Stem Cell Act of 2002, as amended in 2008, allows research on qualifying imported stem cell lines. Such research, however, is strictly regulated and must be approved by an ethics commission.

I. Introduction

Germany permits embryonic stem cell research only on existing stem cell lines imported from abroad. This policy, while reflecting public opinion in Germany, is restrictive in comparison with many other developed nations.[1] Germany's reluctance to permit stem cell research may have developed in reaction to the eugenics policy of the Third Reich when the "unfit" were sterilized or killed and those with the genetic make-up of the "master race" were encouraged to breed.[2] In addition, beginning in the 1980s, Germans developed a skeptical attitude toward technical and scientific progress.[3] The Green Party, as well as conservative politicians, capitalized on these apprehensions and succeeded in facilitating the passage of restrictive legislation on human reproductive technology.[4]

---

[1] Permissive standards for stem cell research are found in the United Kingdom, Japan, and France, whereas Austria, Ireland, and Poland ban all stem cell research. *See* Stephen R. Latham, *SYMPOSIUM: Comparative Health Law and Policy: What, If Anything, Can We Learn from Other Countries?: Between Public Opinion and Public Policy: Human Embryonic Stem-Cell Research and Path-Dependency*, 37 J.L. MED. & ETHICS 800 (2009); *and* J. Robertson, *Reproductive Technology in Germany and the United States: An Essay in Comparative Law and Bioethics*, 43 COLUMJ TRANSNAT'L 189 (2004).

[2] A. Campbell, *Ethos and Economics, Examining the Rationale Underlying Stem Cell and Cloning Research Policies in the United States, Germany, and Japan*, 31 AM. J.L. & MED. 47 (2005).

[3] ERWIN DEUTSCH & ANDREAS SPICKOFF, MEDIZINRECHT 458 (2008).

[4] Robertson, *supra* note 1, at 205.

The constitutional justification for German restrictions on stem cell research is found in the basic rights of human dignity and human life.[5] The statutory bases of the current German policies are the Embryo Protection Act of 1990[6] and the Stem Cell Act of 2002.[7] The former prohibits any embryonic manipulation that does not lead to implantation of the embryo into the womb of its biological mother. The latter permits embryonic stem cell research to a limited extent; as last amended in 2008, it permits the use of imported stem cell lines derived from embryos that were created before May 1, 2007.

II. Constitutional Issues

Article 1(1) of the Basic Law, the German Constitution of 1949, protects human dignity and article 2(2) guarantees the right to life.[8] At least since the 1975 abortion decision of the Federal Constitutional Court,[9] these protections have been deemed applicable to the fetus and have imposed a duty on the state to protect unborn life. The Court, however, balanced the rights of the fetus with the right of personal development of the pregnant woman, and on the basis of this decision, abortion is prohibited in principle, but is permissible if indicated for social or medical reasons, and also during the first trimester of pregnancy after appropriate counseling.[10]

There is much controversy on the extent to which the constitutional protections of the fetus apply to laboratory-created extracorporeal embryos.[11] The opinions range from the protection-worthiness of any embryo, and even any totipotent cell,[12] to denying constitutional protection to in vitro-generated embryos unless nidation has occurred.[13] Nevertheless, there appears to be a strong majority opinion according to which any production or cultivation of human embryos for the purpose of scientific or economic use violates the guarantee of human

---

[5] Grundgesetz für die Bundesrepublik Deutschland [GG], May 23, 1949, BGBL. I, arts. 1(1) and 2(2).

[6] Gesetz zum Schutz von Embryonen [ESchG] [Embryo Protection Act], Dec. 13, 1990, BGBL. I at 2746, as last amended by Gesetz, Nov. 21, 2011, BGBL. I at 2228, *available at* http://www.gesetze-im-internet.de/eschg/index.html, translation of original Act by Auswärtiges Amt, available at http://www.auswaertiges-amt.de/cae/servlet/contentblob/480804/publicationFile/5162/EmbryoProtectionAct.pdf.

[7] Stammzellgesetz [StZG] [Stem Cell Act], June 28, 2002, BGBL. I at 2277, as last amended by Gesetz, Aug. 18, 2008, BGBL. I at 1708, *available at* http://www.gesetze-im-internet.de/stzg/index.html.

[8] GG arts. 1(1) & 2(2).

[9] Decision, Feb. 25, 1975, BVERFGE 39, 1 (1975), translation by Robert E. Jonas & John D. Gorby, 9 THE JOHN MARSHALL JOURNAL OF PRACTICE AND PROCEDURE 605 (1978), *available at.* http://groups.csail.mit.edu/mac/users/rauch/germandecision/german_abortion_decision2_html.

[10] Strafgesetzbuch für die Bundesrepublik Deutschland [StGB] [German Criminal Code], May 15, 1871, repromulgated Nov. 13, 1998 BGBL. I at 3322, as last amended by Gesetz, June 25, 2012, BGBL. at 1374, §§ 218–219, *available at* http://www.gesetze-im-internet.de/stgb/index html, up-to-date English translation *available at* http://www.gesetze-im-internet.de/englisch_stgb/englisch_stgb html#p1784.

[11] Hans Hofmann, *in* BRUNO SCHMIDT-BLEIBTREU ET AL., GRUNDGESETZ KOMMENTAR, GG art. 1 n.30 (2010).

[12] *Id.*

[13] JULIA SCHLÜTER, SCHUTZKONZEPTE FÜR MENSCHLICHE KEIMBAHNZELLEN IN DER FORTPFLANZUNGSMEDIZIN, 175 (2008), reviewed favorably by Rudolf Ratzel, *Sonstiges*, GESUNDHEITSRECHT 222 (2009).

dignity.[14]   The ongoing constitutional debate, therefore, deals primarily with surplus embryos that remain unused in an in vitro fertilization process.

Freedom of scientific research is guaranteed by article 5(3) of the Basic Law. Scientists often insist that this protection has to be taken into consideration when evaluating the constitutional rights of embryos.[15] They also argue that the therapeutic benefits that may result from embryonic stem cell research serve to enhance everyone's human dignity and right to life.[16]

The European Charter of Fundamental Rights[17] also protects human dignity and the right to life, and the Charter has been binding on Germany since December 1, 2009, the effective date stipulated in the Treaty of Lisbon.[18] These protections, however, may not have much impact at present, because the European Union gives member states much freedom in their stem cell research policy.[19] The European Court of Justice, however, has denied patentability to an invention "where the technical teaching which is the subject-matter of the patent application requires the prior destruction of human embryos or their use as base material, whatever the stage at which that takes place and even if the description of the technical teaching claimed does not refer to the use of human embryos."[20]

III. The Embryo Protection Act

The German Embryo Protection Act of 1990[21] severely limits reproductive technology by criminalizing all its uses except for in vitro fertilization leading to the impregnation of the woman from whom the egg originated.[22] Surplus embryos are rarely generated under the German regime because the Act limits the number of embryos that can be generated for each treatment cycle to three and requires that all three be implanted.[23] The creation of embryos for

---

[14] Hofmann, *supra* note 11, art. 2 nn.61 & 62.

[15] Jochen Taupitz, *Embryonenschutz und Stammzellforschung*, BUNDESZENTRALE FÜR POLITISCHE BILDUNG (Jan. 29, 2009), http://www.bpb.de/gesellschaft/umwelt/bioethik/33770/embryonenschutz.

[16] *Id.*

[17] Charter of Fundamental Rights of the European Union arts. 1 & 2, Dec. 18, 2000, 2000 Official Journal of the European Communities (C 364) 1, http://www.europarl.europa.eu/charter/pdf/text_en.pdf.

[18] Treaty of Lisbon, Amending the Treaty on the European Union and the Treaty Establishing the European Communities, Dec. 13, 2007, 2007 O.J. (C 306) 1. http://eur-lex.europa.eu/JOHtml.do?uri=OJ.C.2007:306: SOM:EN:HTML.

[19] DIRK CIPER ET AL., MEDIZINRECHT 584 (2012).

[20] Case C-34/10, Oliver Brüstle v. Greenpeace e.V., Eur. Ct. J. (Oct. 18, 2011),http://eur-lex.europa.eu/LexUriServ/LexUriServ.do?uri=CELEX:62010CJ0034:EN:HTML.

[21] ESchG, *supra* note 6.

[22] A narrow exception from this principle was recently enacted to allow pre-implantation genetic diagnosis in the course of in vitro fertilization if a parent has a genetic predisposition for a serious hereditary disease. ESchG § 3a, as introduced by Präimplantationsdiagnostikgesetz, Nov. 21, 2011. BGBL. I at 2228.

[23] ESchG § 1.

research purposes is prohibited[24] as is the creation of embryos through therapeutic cloning or parthenogenesis.[25]

In addition to preventing the creation of a supply of embryos that could be used for the harvesting of stem cells, the Embryo Protection Act prohibits any use of the embryo that does not serve the purpose of its preservation.[26] The Act defines "embryo" in section 8, which translates as follows:

> (1) For the purpose of this Act, an embryo already means the human egg cell, fertilised and capable of developing, from the time of fusion of the nuclei, and further, each totipotent cell removed from an embryo that is assumed to be able to divide and to develop into an individual under the appropriate conditions for that.
> (2) In the first twenty-four hours after nuclear fusion, the fertilised human egg cell is held to [be] capable of development except when it is established before expiry of this time period that it will not develop beyond the one-cell stage.
> (3) Germ line cells, for the purpose of this Act, are all cells that lead of the egg and sperm cells to the resultant human being and, further, the egg cell from capture or penetration of the sperm cell until the end of fertilisation by fusion of the nuclei.[27]

The Act thereby effectively prohibits the creation of stem cells from German embryos, and it sanctions violations with one to five years' imprisonment,[28] yet it does not specifically prohibit stem cell research: an alteration of germ line cells is not prohibited if it is carried out on cells that will not be transferred to an embryo, fetus, or human being, and will not lead to the origination of a germ cell.[29]

IV. The Stem Cell Act

The Stem Cell Act of June 2002 aimed to give German scientists an opportunity to conduct embryonic stem cell research. For this purpose, the Act permits the importation of stem cells, provided they were derived from surplus embryos that were not defective and were intended to be used for reproductive purposes but were not used in this manner.[30] Further requirements for importation are compliance with the laws of the country of origin and the absence of any pecuniary compensation.[31]

---

[24] *Id.*

[25] ESchG § 6.

[26] ESchG § 2.

[27] Copied from translation of Auswärtiges Amt, *supra* note 6.

[28] ESchG §§ 1, 2, 4–7 & 11.

[29] ESchG § 5, ¶ 2. *See also* M. BREWE, EMBRYONENSCHUTZ UND STAMMZELLENGESETZ 34 (Berlin, 2006).

[30] StZG § 1.

[31] *Id.*

As originally enacted, the Act permitted the importation of stem cells only if they were derived from embryos that were created prior to January 1, 2002.[32] This time limit intended to ensure that Germany would only import already existing stem cells and that German demands would not encourage the harvesting of stem cells in other countries.[33] In 2008, this time limit was extended to May 1, 2007.[34] This was deemed necessary to provide for a new supply of stem cell lines. At the same time, the Act was amended by limiting its scope of application to embryonic stem cell research carried out in Germany,[35] to ensure that German scientists would not be criminally liable for participating in international research endeavors.

The decision to extend the deadline was reached after an extensive debate in Parliament that showed how divided Germans are on this issue.[36] Four different drafts were under discussion. These ranged from proposing a total prohibition on embryonic stem cell research to proposing the elimination of any limiting dates for foreign stem cell lines.[37]

The Stem Cell Act does not free German scientists from the limitations of the Embryo Protection Act nor from the governance of a regulatory regime. To ensure compliance with the law, research projects must obtain a license from the designated authority, currently the Robert Koch Institute,[38] and to review the ethical aspects of research applications, an Ethics Commission has been created that consist of biologists, physicians, ethicists, and theologians.[39] Licenses will be granted only for research projects that serve goals of ethically high standing, and that are limited to basic and therapeutic research for which human stem cell research is indispensable.[40]

The executive branch of the German government informs Parliament and the public biannually of the stem cell research that has been carried out in Germany. The latest report was published in February 2011.[41] It covers the period 2008 through 2009 and reveals that nine requests for the importation of embryonic stem cells were submitted during the period covered by the report, and that these requests dealt primarily with basic research for the long-term goal of developing diagnostic, preventive, or therapeutic procedures. The report also indicated satisfaction in the scientific community over the 2008 amendments of the Stem Cell Act.

---

[32] StZG § 4, as originally enacted.

[33] StZG § 1.

[34] StZG § 4, as amended by Gesetz, Aug. 14, 2008, BGBL. I at 1708.

[35] StZG § 2, as amended by Gesetz, Aug. 14, 2008, BGBL. I at 1708.

[36] Deutscher Bundestag, Plenarprotokoll 16/142, Feb. 14, 2008.

[37] *Id.*

[38] The Robert Koch Institute, http://www.rki.de/, is the German agency for disease control and related matters.

[39] StZG §§ 6-9.

[40] StZG § 5.

[41] Deutscher Bundestag, *Unterrichtung*, Feb. 10, 2011, Drucksache 17/4760 http://dip21.bundestag.de/dip21/btd/17/047/1704760.pdf.

V. Conclusion

German legislation attempts to bridge a seemingly irreconcilable clash of opinions between the proponents of ethical limits and the interests of scientists to remain competitive in biomedical research. It is a matter of opinion whether the current solution succeeds in balancing these contradictory goals. Whereas scientists approve of the now existing feasibility of stem cell research,[42] critics continue to deem it unethical and of unproven therapeutic value.[43]

Prepared by Edith Palmer, Chief
Foreign, Comparative and
International Law Division II
With the assistance of Sophia Schick,
Interning Law Specialist
September 2012

---

[42] *Id.*

[43] Friedrich Graf von Westphalen, *Das Bild des Menschen im Recht*, ANWALTSBLATT 821 (2009).

LAW LIBRARY OF CONGRESS

JAPAN

PROMOTION AND REGULATION OF BIOTECHNOLOGY

Executive Summary

Japan has developed policies aimed at the promotion of biotechnology and has also enacted bioethics regulations related to different areas of research. The Council for Science and Technology Policy oversees Japan's science and technology policy and formulates comprehensive and basic policies. In addition, the Ministry of Education, Culture, Sports, Science and Technology has a Council for Science and Technology that carries out research and deliberations relating to the promotion of science and technology. Branches of these councils deliberate on bioethics issues, and the government decides on policies and regulations based on their advice. Guidelines on ethics in human genome and gene analysis research are currently being revised by some of these entities, including in relation to privacy and consent requirements.

I. Regulatory Framework

Japan enacted the Science and Technology Basic Law in 1995.[1] This law prescribes the basic policy requirements for the promotion of science and technology. It also comprehensively and systematically promotes the development of policies for the advancement of science and technology.[2] The law requires the government to prepare a Science and Technology Basic Plan every five years.[3] In 2001, Japan established the Council for Science and Technology Policy (CSTP) in the Cabinet Office as one of the policy councils that work on key policy areas. The CSTP oversees the nation's science and technology policy, formulates comprehensive and basic policies, and is responsible for their overall coordination.[4] When the government draws up the Science and Technology Basic Plan, it must consult with the CSTP.[5]

---

[1] The Science and Technology Basic Law, Act No. 130 of 1995, English translation *available at* the Cabinet Office's website, http://www8.cao.go.jp/cstp/english/law/index.html (last visited Aug. 15, 2012).

[2] *Id.* art. 1.

[3] *Id.* art. 9.

[4] CABINET OFFICE, COUNCIL FOR SCIENCE AND TECHNOLOGY POLICY 1, http://www8.cao.go.jp/cstp/english/panhu/index.html (click "p1 Introduction, Overview of the Council for Science and Technology Policy") (last visited Sept. 5, 2012).

[5] The Science and Technology Basic Law, art. 9, ¶ 3.

The fourth Science and Technology Basic Plan was issued in August 2011.[6] The plan identifies the most important agenda items for the next five years as reconstruction and rebuilding from the earthquake disaster, promoting innovation in green technologies, and promoting "life innovation."[7] The Japanese government uses the phrase "life innovation" to mean innovations in the fields of medical, daily life assistance, and wellness care.[8] Within the life innovation field, the government targets genome sequencing analysis, induced pluripotent stem (iPS) cell medical treatments, and regenerative medicine.[9]

The life sciences field has been one of most significant areas that the government has promoted since the second Basic Plan.[10] Because it considers that the development of biotechnology is especially important, in 2002 the government also established the Biotechnology Strategy Council to advance a biotechnology development strategy for Japan.[11] The Biotechnology Strategy Council issued the Biotechnology Strategy Guidelines in December 2002.[12] The Biotechnology Strategy Council was transformed into the Public-Private Joint Committee for Strategic Promotion of Biotechnology in 2008.[13] In December 2008, the Joint Committee released new guidelines for Japan's biotechnology strategies called "Dream BT [Biotechnology] Japan."[14]

The Ministry of Education, Culture, Sports, Science and Technology (MEXT) also has a Council, the Council for Science and Technology (CST), which "carries out research and deliberation on important matters relating to the promotion of science and technology."[15] The Council's Subdivision on Research Planning and Evaluation has a Life Science Committee within it.[16]

---

[6] Kagaku gijutsu kihon keikaku [Science and Technology Basic Plan], Cabinet Decision (Aug. 19, 2011), http://www8.cao.go.jp/cstp/kihonkeikaku/4honbun.pdf.

[7] *Id.* at 8.

[8] *Id.*

[9] *Id.* at 14.

[10] Science and Technology Basic Plan, Cabinet Decision (Mar. 28, 2006), at 17, http://www8.cao.go.jp/cstp/english/basic/3rd-Basic-Plan-rev.pdf.

[11] Concerning the Biotechnology Strategy Council, Prime Minister's Decision (July 5, 2002), http://www.kantei.go.jp/foreign/policy/bt/konkyo_e.html.

[12] Biotechnology Strategy Guidelines (Draft) (Dec. 6, 2002), English translation *available at* Japan Bioindustry Association's website, http://www.jba.or.jp/jabex/pdf/BT%20Strategy%20Guideline%20(translated%20by%20JETRO).pdf.

[13] Public-Private Joint Committee for Strategic Promotion of Biotechnology, Minutes of the First Meeting (Mar. 17, 2008), at 1, http://www8.cao.go.jp/cstp/project/bt2/haihu1/giji1.pdf.

[14] Public-Private Joint Committee for Strategic Promotion of Biotechnology, Dorīmu BT Japan [Dream BT Japan] (Dec. 2008), http://www8.cao.go.jp/cstp/project/bt2/bt_01-08.pdf.

[15] *National Councils*, MEXT, http://www.mext.go.jp/english/organization/1303054.htm (last visited Sept. 5, 2012).

[16] *Kenkyū keikaku/ hyōka bunka kai [Subdivision on Research Planning and Evaluation]*, MEXT, http://www.mext.go.jp/b_menu/shingi/gijyutu/gijyutu2/index.html (last visited Sept. 5, 2012).

In 2001, the CSTP established the Expert Panel on Bioethics to investigate and study ethical issues in the life sciences.[17]   There is also a component of the CST known as the Subdivision on Bioethics/Safety.[18]

The CSTP Expert Panel aims to provide basic direction on bioethics issues. It submits its opinions to the Prime Minister or the relevant minister(s). The CST Subdivision researches and discusses the administration of ethical guidelines within MEXT and other ethical matters important for MEXT. The CSTP Expert Panel and the CST Subdivision are expected to communicate with each other.[19]   The fifteen expert members of the CSTP Expert Panel mostly consist of university professors in the fields of science, medicine, and law. There are a few from research institutions, one from a private company, and one from the media.[20]   The twenty-one members of the CST Subdivision have a similar background, but there is more variety. More than half are professors, but several are from medical and research institutions. One is from a pharmaceutical industry association and one is from a medical doctors' association.[21]

Based on the work of the CSTP and other councils and panels, the government has enacted laws that include regulations on ethical issues in specific areas of research, and has issued various ethical guidelines, including on biotechnology. For example, Japan enacted the Act on Regulation of Human Cloning Techniques in 2000 that obligates MEXT to establish guidelines on the handling of specified embryos,[22] which MEXT subsequently issued in 2001.[23] The Ministry of Health and Welfare devised the Guidelines on Gene Therapy Clinical Study in 1994[24] and, with MEXT, made amendments and issued new Guidelines in 2002.[25]

---

[17] *Plenary Meeting & Expert Panel*, BUREAU OF SCIENCE AND TECHNOLOGY POLICY, CABINET OFFICE, http://www8.cao.go.jp/cstp/english/policy/panel.html (last visited Sept. 5, 2012).

[18] *Seimeirinri/ anzen bukai [Subdivision on Bioethics/Safety]*, MEXT, http://www.mext.go.jp/b_menu/shingi/gijyutu/gijyutu1/index.htm (last visited Sept. 5, 2012).

[19] *Seimei rinri/ anzen bukai ni tsuite [Regarding Council on Bioethics/Safety]*, MEXT (Mar. 15, 2001), http://www.mext.go.jp/b_menu/shingi/gijyutu/gijyutu1/gaiyou/010301.htm.

[20] Sōgō kagaku gijutsu kaigi seimei rinri senmon chōsakai meibo [Member list of CSTP Expert Panel on Bioethics] (Apr. 1, 2012), http://www8.cao.go.jp/cstp/tyousakai/life/lifemember.pdf.

[21] Seimei rinri anzen bukai iin meibo [Bioethics·Safety Subdivision, Member List], MEXT (May 2005), http://www.mext.go.jp/b_menu/shingi/gijyutu/gijyutu1/meibo/010301.htm.

[22] Hito ni kansuru kuron gijutsu to no kisei ni kansuru horitsu [Act on Regulation of Human Cloning Techniques], Act No. 146 of 2000, art. 4, English translation *available at* MEXT website, http://www.cas.go.jp/jp/seisaku/hourei/data/htc.pdf.

[23] Tokutei hai no toriatsukai ni kansuru shishin [Guidelines for Handling of a Specified Embryo], MEXT Notification No. 173 of 2001, English translation *available at* MEXT website, http://www.lifescience.mext.go.jp/files/pdf/30_82.pdf.

[24] Annual Health, Labour and Welfare Report, MHLW, at 259 (2010), http://www.mhlw.go.jp/english/wp/wp-hw4/dl/health_science/2011071902.pdf. The full annual report may be viewed at http://www.mhlw.go.jp/english/wp/wp-hw4/index.html.

[25] Idenshi chiryō rinsh kenku ni kansuru shishin [Indicator on the gene therapy clinical study], MEXT & MHLW Notification No. 1 (Mar. 27, 2002), http://www.mhlw.go.jp/general/seido/kousei/i-kenkyu/idenshi/0504sisin.html.

II. Current Issue: Privacy and Consent in Human Genome and Gene Analysis Research

Various councils and panels have regularly discussed issues in biotechnology. Currently, one of the important topics concerns an amendment to the ethical guidelines on the study of the human genome and gene analysis. In 2000, the Bioethics Committee of the CST released the Fundamental Principles of Research on the Human Genome.[26] Based on this, in 2001, MEXT, the Ministry of Health, Labour and Welfare (MHLW), and the Ministry of Economy, Trade and Industry (METI) issued the Ethics Guidelines on Human Genome and Gene Analysis Research (hereinafter "Guidelines").[27]

The Guidelines seek to protect human dignity and human rights and ensure that research will be promoted properly based on the understanding and cooperation of society.[28] Under the Guidelines, a research institution that conducts human genome research must establish an Ethics Review Committee within the institution.[29] The Ethics Review Committee examines a research protocol from an ethical and scientific viewpoint and conveys its opinions to the director of the institution.[30] When the Ethics Review Committee does not approve the research protocol, the director of the institution cannot allow researchers to conduct the protocol.[31] The principal researcher also must report the progress of human genome/gene analysis research to the director of their research institution at least annually.[32]

The Guidelines emphasize the importance of giving an adequate prior explanation to a donor and obtaining informed consent based on his/her free will.[33] The principal researcher of a research project must inform a donor, in advance, of the significance, objective(s), method and expected results of research, any disadvantage to the donor that might incur, and the method of preservation and use of human specimens.[34]

The Guidelines also take into account the special privacy considerations that arise in relation to human genetic information. As revealing an individual's genetic information would also reveal his/her biological family members' genetic information, it is important that the

---

[26] Hito genomu kenkyu ni kansuru kihon gensoku nit suite [Fundamental Principles of Research on the Human Genome], Bioethics Committee, CST (June 14, 2000), http://www.lifescience mext.go.jp/files/pdf/43 136.pdf, English translation *available at* http://www.lifescience mext.go.jp/files/pdf/43 137.pdf.

[27] Hito genomu idenshi kaiseki kenkyu ni kansuru rinri shishin [Ethics Guidelines for Human Genome and Gene Analysis Research], MEXT, MHLW, & METI Notification No. 1 (Mar. 29, 2001), http://www.lifescience mext.go.jp/files/pdf/40 211.pdf, English translation *available at* http://www.lifescience mext.go.jp/files/pdf/40 213.pdf.

[28] *Id.* at Pt. I, 1.

[29] *Id.* at Pt. II, 4(4) (currently Pt. II, 6(8)).

[30] *Id.* at Pt. II, 7(1) (currently Pt. II, 9(1)).

[31] *Id.* at Pt. II, 4(5) (currently Pt. II, 6(9)).

[32] *Id.* at Pt. II, 5(5) (currently Pt. II, 7(5)).

[33] *Id.* at Pt. I, 1(2).

[34] *Id.* at Pt. III, 8(2) (currently Pt. III, 10(3)).

information is properly protected. Also, genetic information may reveal a higher possibility of future health problems of the person, and some people may not want to know such negative information. There is also a risk that insurance companies or employers could use genetic information to treat job applicants unfairly.[35]

The current Guidelines contain various provisions relating to the protection of the personal information of donors. The director of the research institution must appoint a personal information custodian.[36] A personal information custodian or a researcher must render donors' information anonymous before the research is undertaken.[37] When a donor requests his/her own genetic information that was revealed by the research to be disclosed, the principal researcher must do so.[38] The Guidelines were amended in 2004[39] to incorporate policies and procedures to enhance protection of personal information that were required under the Act on Protection of Personal Information that was enacted in 2003.[40] Also, guidelines on the utilization of specimens that had been provided before the institution planned human genome research were supplemented.[41]

MEXT, MHLW and METI started considering amending the Guidelines in 2011 in order to take into account recent developments, particularly the fact that researchers now deal with a large quantity of genetic information in order to determine relationships between diseases and genes, as well as improvements in the methods and speed of analysis. Each ministry's committee responsible for the Guidelines began to hold joint meetings in April 2011.[42] The joint committee drafted revised Guidelines and asked for public comment on them in February 2012.[43] The following are examples of proposed revisions.

One of the revisions concerns utilization of specimens that had been donated before a human genome research was planned. The current Guidelines basically require researchers to obtain donors' consent before they use such specimens. While in cases where the donor's

---

[35] Minutes of the first meeting, Human genome research sub-committee, MEXT (Jan. 28, 2000), http://www mext.go.jp/b_menu/shingi/kagaku/rinri/hitogeg1 htm.

[36] *Id.* at Pt. II, 4(3) (currently Pt. II, 6(7)).

[37] *Id.* at Pt. II, 6(1) (currently Pt. II, 8(1)).

[38] *Id.* at Pt. III, 9(1) (currently Pt. II, 11(1)).

[39] MEXT, MHLW & METI Notification No. 1 (Dec. 28, 2004), English translation *available at* http://www.lifescience.mext.go.jp/files/pdf/n796_00.pdf.

[40] Act on Protection of Personal Information, Act No. 57 of 2003.

[41] Ethics Guidelines for Human Genome and Gene Analysis Research, MEXT, MHLW, METI Notification No. 1 (Mar. 29, 2001), *amended by* MEXT, MHLW & METI Notification No. 1 (Dec. 28, 2004), Pt. IV, 13.

[42] "Hito genomu idenshi kaiseki kenkyū ni kansuru rinri shishin" no minaosi ni tsuite (an) [Regarding the review of the Ethics Guidelines on Human Genome and Gene Analysis Research (proposal)], MEXT, MHLW & METI (Feb. 3, 2012), http://www.lifescience.mext.go.jp/files/pdf/n979_01.pdf.

[43] "Hito genomu idenshi kaiseki kenkyū ni kansuru rinri shishin" no minaosi ni kansuru iken boshū no jisshi ni tsuite [Regarding acceptance of opinions on the review of the Ethics Guidelines on Human Genome and Gene Analysis Research], E-GOV, http://search.e-gov.go.jp/servlet/Public?CLASSNAME=PCMMSTDETAIL&id=185000561&Mode=0 (last visited Sept. 5, 2012).

identity has been disconnected to the specimen, it can be utilized for human genome research upon the approvals of the Ethics Review Committee and the director of the institution, in cases where the specimen is not disconnected to information that can identify the donor, utilization of the specimen for human genome research is limited.[44]   The proposed revision expands the exceptions.[45]   For example, in the case of a specimen for which the donor's identity could be connected by a donor-specimen chart, but the chart is not available, the researchers may utilize the specimen for human genome research by making research information available to donor groups or the public.[46]

The current Guidelines have a provision concerning cases in which a research institution transfers specimens to a human cell/gene/specimen bank.   In such cases, the transferring institution must disconnect the donor's information from the specimen and follow the terms of the donor's consent agreement.[47]   However, the Guidelines do not have provisions regarding the procedure and criteria for transfer of specimens or research information from one research institution to another.   A proposed revision adds these.[48]   The proposed revision mandates that the transferring institution let the recipient institution know the terms of the donor's consent agreement.   The transferring institution must disconnect donor identity information from specimens or research information.   However, if the donor has agreed to a transfer and the Ethics Committee approves it, the transferring institution can transfer the specimen or research information to another research institution without disconnecting the donor's identity information.[49]

Prepared by Sayuri Umeda
Senior Foreign Law Specialist
September 2012

---

[44] Ethics Guidelines for Human Genome and Gene Analysis Research, MEXT, MHLW, METI Notification No. 1 (Mar. 29, 2001), *last amended by* MEXT, MHLW & METI Notification No. 1 (Dec. 1, 2008), Pt. IV, 13.

[45] Regarding the Review of the Ethics Guidelines on Human Genome and Gene Analysis Research (proposal), *supra* note 43, at 3(1).

[46] "Hito genomu idenshi kaiseki kenkyū ni kansuru rinri shishin" no minaosi an [Review of the Ethics Guidelines on Human Genome and Gene Analysis Research (proposal)], MEXT, MHLW & METI, proposed Pt. V, 14, at 52-53, http://www.lifescience.mext.go.jp/files/pdf/n979_02.pdf.

[47] Ethics Guidelines for Human Genome and Gene Analysis Research, MEXT, MHLW, & METI Notification No. 1 (Mar. 29, 2001), *last amended by* MEXT, MHLW & METI Notification No. 1 (Dec. 1, 2008), Pt. IV, 14(2).

[48] Regarding the Review of the Ethics Guidelines on Human Genome and Gene Analysis Research (proposal), *supra* note 42, at 3(2).

[49] Review of the Ethics Guidelines on Human Genome and Gene Analysis Research (proposal), *supra* note 47, proposed Pt. V, 11, at 49.

LAW LIBRARY OF CONGRESS

CHINA

EMBRYONIC STEM CELL RESEARCH AND POPULATION CONTROL

Executive Summary

In China, embryonic stem cells from specified sources are allowed to be used in research, including unwanted gametes or blastulas from in vitro fertilization (IVF) procedures, embryo cells from miscarriages or voluntarily induced abortions, blastulas or single split blastocysts from somatic cell nuclear transfer technology, or donated germ cells. Embryos cultured in vitro may not be developed exceeding 14 days. Implantation of human blastulas back into a human or animal's reproductive system, and the combination of human germ cells with those of other species is strictly prohibited.

Given that population control is a fundamental State policy, abortion is generally permitted but limited by a ban on sex-selective abortions. The number of abortions performed each year is high. In response to the increasingly imbalanced sex ratio, the government prohibits hospitals and doctors from disclosing the gender of a fetus to the parents and from performing sex-selective abortions. Because of the birth limit couples who have had successful IVF may not use the leftover embryos for a future pregnancy, and according to the ethical principles of assisted reproductive technology (ART) they may not be able to donate them to other infertile couples. In addition, the law and policy related to the population control policy have the potential to create an abundance of embryonic bodies for stem cell research.

I. Background

In recent decades, the Chinese government has been placing great emphasis on science and technology, as it is seen as crucial for China's economic growth and sustainable development. Stem cell research has been specifically prioritized as a field in which there is potential for China to successfully compete with developed countries. The country's leaders have repeatedly stressed the importance of stem cell research and stem cell treatment. In a statement made in 2009, Premiere Wen Jiabao stated that

[s]tem cell research promotes the development of regenerative medicine, which is another revolutionary progress following drug treatment and surgical treatment. We must strive to gain a leading position in more areas of stem cell research. In the meantime, great

importance and caution should be attached to the ethical issues arising from stem cell research.[1]

While ethical issues are being noted and addressed in government instruments and official regulations, China continues to have one of the most unrestrictive regulatory regimes on stem cell research. Chinese law and policy are also known to be liberal with regard to abortion, which, together with the overall population control policy and its implementation, is another major area where bioethical issues may arise. This report addresses (1) the regulatory framework regarding embryonic stem cell research; and (2) the law and policy on population control and human reproduction and their possible effect on the embryonic stem cell research.

II. Embryonic Stem Cell Research

For more than half a century (since 1949), China has been under the leadership of the Communist Party of China (CPC), which is officially atheist. The history of regulatory control of biotechnology in China is not long. Some scientists have advocated that there should be no constraint whatsoever on stem cell research in order to ensure the advancement of science and technology.[2] With research interest in this area increasing, the government has started to regulate it by incorporating "international ethical guidelines" of respecting life and patients' rights and welfare.[3] Still, China has not passed any national law regulating this area; relevant regulations are mainly found in the guidelines issued by the central government ministries.

A. Ethical Guidelines for Embryonic Stem Cell Research

In 2003, the Ministry of Science and Technology (MOST) and the Ministry of Health (MOH) jointly issued a set of ethical guidelines specifically regulating human embryonic stem cell research, the Guidelines for Ethical Principles in Human Embryonic Stem Cell Research (hereinafter Guidelines).[4] The purposes of the Guidelines are twofold: to "ensure the observance of the internationally recognized life ethical principles and relevant domestic regulations," and to "promote healthy development of human embryonic stem cell research."[5]

---

[1] Wen Jiabao, *Rang Keji Yinling Zhongguo Ke Chixu Fazhan* [*Let Science and Technology Leads China's Sustainable Development*], CENTRAL PEOPLE'S GOVERNMENT (Nov. 3, 2009), http://www.gov.cn/ldhd/2009-11/23/content_1471208.htm (in Chinese; translation by the author).

[2] Qiu Renzong, *China Taking the Right Steps in Bioethics*, SCIDEV NET (May 18, 2007), http://www.scidev.net/en/opinions/china-taking-the-right-steps-in-bioethics.html.

[3] *Id.* Whether there are universally applicable ethical guidelines in this area is in fact arguable; rather, the concept was referred to when advocating for a right to life, and it seems to have been somewhat accepted by government rule makers.

[4] Ren Peitai Ganxibao Yanjiu Lunli Zhidao Yuanze [Guidelines for Ethical Principles in Human Embryonic Stem Cell Research] (Guo Ke Fa Sheng Zi [2003] No. 460, promulgated by the MOST and MOH on Dec. 24, 2003), http://www.most.gov.cn/fggw/zfwj/zfwj2003/200512/t20051214_54948.htm (in Chinese). An English translation is provided by WESTLAWCHINA.COM (by subscription), which is used with some amendments by the author when referred to in this report.

[5] *Id.* art. 1.

According to the Guidelines, embryonic stem cells from specified sources are allowed to be used in research, including unwanted gametes or blastulas from in vitro fertilization (IVF) procedures, embryo cells from miscarriages or voluntarily induced abortions, blastulas or single split blastocysts from somatic cell nuclear transfer technology, or donated germ cells.[6] Where blastula is obtained from external fertilization, somatic nucleus transplantation, unisexual duplicating technique or genetic modification, the culture period in vitro shall not exceed fourteen days from the day of fecundation or nuclear transplantation.[7]

Research aimed at human reproductive cloning is strictly prohibited.[8] Buying or selling human gametes, cytulas, embryos, or embryonic tissue is forbidden by the Guidelines.[9] Embryonic stem cell research is subject to review by an ethics committee within the researcher's own institution: according to the Guidelines, hospitals and research institutions engaging in embryonic stem cell research must establish institutional ethics committees that consist of research and executive personnel in the areas of biology, medical science, law, and social sciences.[10]

The Guidelines strictly prohibit implantation of human blastulas back into a human or animal's reproductive system. Also, combining human germ cells with those of other species is prohibited.[11] One scholar has noted, however, that this provision actually permits the procurement of stem cells from hybrid human-animal embryos, as it permits the fusion of human cell nuclei with enucleated egg cells from animals, which makes China one of only two countries in the world, along with the United Kingdom, that allow research on the creation of cytoplasmic hybrid embryos.[12]

B. Recent Developments in Regulatory Control of Stem Cell Treatment

The Chinese government appears to be considering tighter regulation over stem cell treatment. On December 16, 2011, the MOH circulated a notice ordering an immediate halt to unapproved stem cell treatments and putting the receipt of applications for new projects on hold until July 1, 2012.[13] Although July 1 has now passed, it appears that the MOH has not resumed accepting new applications. According to an MOH spokesman, all stem cell research projects

---

[6] *Id.* art. 5.

[7] *Id.* art. 6.

[8] *Id.* art. 4.

[9] *Id.* art. 7.

[10] *Id.* art. 9.

[11] *Id.* art. 6.

[12] Kerstin Klein, *Illiberal Biopolitics and 'Embryonic Life': The Governance of Human Embryonic Stem Cell Research in China, in* THE RIGHT TO LIFE AND THE VALUE OF LIFE: ORIENTATIONS IN LAW, POLITICS AND ETHICS 411 (Jon Yorke ed., 2010).

[13] Guanyu Kaizhan Ganxibao Linchuang Yanjiu he Yingyong Zi Cha Zijiu Gongzuo de Tongzhi [Notice on Carrying Out Self-Inspection and Self-Correction in Stem Cell Treatment Research and Application] (Wei Ban Ke Jiao Han [2011] No. 1177 (MOH, Dec. 16, 2011), http://www.moh.gov.cn/publicfiles/business/htmlfiles/mohkjjys/s3582/201201/53890.htm (in Chinese).

that have been approved are now been reviewed "very strictly" for recertification. The spokesman indicated that MOH has joined with the State Food and Drug Administration (SFDA) to develop two new comprehensive rules regulating research on stem cell treatment.[14]

III. Law and Policy on Population Control and Human Reproduction

A. 'One-Child Policy'

China's current population control policy, commonly known as the "one-child policy," was formally introduced in the late 1970s and remains in force. That policy, which limits most married couples in urban areas to bearing one child, allows those in rural areas to bear a second child if their first child is female, among other prescribed exceptions made by local government authorities that apply to their respective jurisdictions.[15]

The policy has been written into the Constitution, which provides that "[t]he State promotes family planning so that population growth may fit the plans for economic and social development."[16] The Population and Family Planning Law (hereinafter Family Planning Law) further specifies that family planning is a "fundamental State policy" for this populous country, and that the State may adopt "comprehensive measures" to control population growth.[17] According to the Law, the State relies on advances in science and technology and a reward system, among other things, in implementing the policy.[18]

1. Birth Control

Given that controlling population growth is a fundamental State policy, abortion law is generally permissive in China, with some restrictions arising from a ban on sex-selective abortion. For "out-of-plan" pregnancies that exceed the birth limit abortion may be encouraged, and is reportedly mandatory in some cases.[19] The State provides universal access to contraception and other birth control services, which may include free contraceptives, sterilization surgeries, and artificial termination of pregnancies.[20] Citizens subject to long-term contraception, sterilization, and artificial abortion will be granted paid leave and may receive rewards from their local government.[21] The official data published by the Ministry of Health

---

[14] Xu Jing, Weishengbu: Jiang Zhengdui Ganxibao Yanjiu Zaifa Wenjian, Yingyong Shangwei Pizhun [Ministry of Health: Documents to be Issued on Stem Cell Research; Clinical Applications Have Not Been Approved], CAIJING (July 9, 2012), http://industry.caijing.com.cn/2012-07-09/111936785.html (in Chinese).

[15] Renkou Yu Jihuashengyu Fa [Law on Population and Family Planning] (promulgated by the Standing Committee of the National People's Congress, Dec. 29, 2001; effective Sept. 1, 2002), art. 18, 13 THE LAWS OF THE PEOPLE'S REPUBLIC OF CHINA (P.R.C. LAWS) (2001) 351, 354.

[16] XIANFA [CONSTITUTION] (1982), art. 25, 16 P.R.C. LAWS (2004) 3, 13 (2005) (translation by the author).

[17] Family Planning Law art. 2, 13 P.R.C. LAWS (2001) 351 (2002).

[18] *Id.*

[19] CONGRESSIONAL-EXECUTIVE COMMISSION ON CHINA (CECC), ANNUAL REPORT 2011 at 110, http://www.cecc.gov/ pages/annualRpt/annualRpt11/AR2011final.pdf.

[20] Family Planning Law art. 21, 13 P.R.C. LAWS (2001) 351, 355 (2002).

[21] *Id.* art. 26, 13 P.R.C. LAWS at 356.

shows a high rate of artificial abortions, ranging from six million to nine million annually in recent years.[22]

2. Gender Determination and Sex-selective Abortion

In 2002, the State Commission for Population and Family Planning, in conjunction with the MOH and SFDA, issued a document prohibiting hospitals and doctors from disclosing the gender of fetuses to the parents and performing sex-selective artificial terminations of pregnancy.[23] Pharmacies are now prohibited from selling pregnancy termination medicines.[24] Although the order was aimed at cracking down on sex-selective abortions, it in fact restricts the termination of pregnancies within the birth limit after fourteen weeks; such terminations must now be approved by the local family planning authority.[25]

The ban on gender determination and sex-selective abortion appears be a response of the government to the increasingly imbalanced sex ratio. China is reported to have the highest sex ratio of males to females in the world, which is arguably due to enforcement of the population control policy: in keeping with the traditional preference for boys and being limited by the one child policy, some parents, in particular those in rural areas whose first child is a girl, may decide to practice sex-selective abortion in order to have another child in an attempt to get a son.[26]

3. Assisted Reproductive Technology and Surrogacy

Surrogacy of any kind is officially prohibited in China. In keeping with the population control policy, single women and couples trying to have an "out-of-plan" child cannot be treated with assisted reproductive technology (ART). These provisions derive from a 2001 MOH order regulating ART (ART Order) and a set of ethical principles for ART and sperm banks that the MOH revised and issued in 2003 (ART Ethical Principles).[27]

---

[22] MINISTRY OF HEALTH OF CHINA, 2010 STATISTIC YEARBOOK OF HYGIENE IN CHINA § 7-6-1, http://www.moh.gov.cn/publicfiles/business/htmlfiles/zwgkzt/ptjnj/year2010/index2010.html (in Chinese; last visited Sept. 10, 2012).

[23] Guanyu Jinzhi Fei yixue Xuyao de Tai'er Xingbie Jianding he Xuanze Xingbie de Rengong Zhongzhi Renshen de Guiding [Regulations Regarding the Prohibition of Non-medically Necessary Gender Determination Examinations and Sex-Selective Termination of Pregnancy (issued by the State Commission for Population and Family Planning, MOH, and SFDA on Nov. 29, 2002, effective Jan. 1, 2003), art. 3, http://www.gov.cn/banshi/2005-10/24/content_82759.htm (in Chinese; last visited Sept. 10, 2012).

[24] *Id.* art. 10.

[25] *Id.* art. 7. Previously, the 2001 Family Planning Law contained a general article prohibiting the use of ultrasonography or other techniques to determine the gender of the fetus, and sex-selective pregnancy termination for non-medical reasons, without specifying the detailed requirements. Family Planning Law art. 35, 13 P.R.C. LAWS (2001) 351, 357 (2002). A similar general provision is found in the 1994 Law on Maternal and Infant Health Care. *See* Mu Ying Bao Jian Fa [Law on Maternal and Infant Health Care] (promulgated by the NPC Standing Committee on Oct. 27, 1994, effective June 1, 1995), art. 32(2), 6 P.R.C. LAWS (1994) 121, 126.

[26] CECC 2011 ANNUAL REPORT, *supra* note 19, at 115.

[27] Renlei Fuzhu Shengzhi Jishu Guanli Banfa [Administrative Measures on Assisted Human Reproduction Technology] (MOH Order [2001] No. 14, effective Aug. 1, 2001) (hereinafter ART Order), art. 3, 6 STATE COUNCIL GAZETTE (STATE COUNCIL GAZ.) 2002, 25–26 (in Chinese); Renlei Fuzhu Shengzhi Jishu he Renlei Jingzi Ku Lunli Yuanze [Ethical Principles of Assisted Human Reproduction Technology and Human Sperm Bank] (Wei Ke Jiao Fa

According to the ART Order, performance of any ART must serve the purpose of medical treatment and is subject to the country's population control policy and ethical principles, as well relevant laws and regulations, and ART may only be performed in officially established medical institutions.[28] Buying or selling gametes, zygotes, or embryos is prohibited.[29] Each medical institution performing ART is required to establish a medical ethics committee to review the ethical issues arises from ART.[30] The Order also requires patients to give their written consent.[31] Medical institutions are required to provide ethical training to the personnel performing ART.[32]

B. Sourcing of Embryos for Human Embryonic Stem Cell Research

One important issue in the advancement of embryonic stem cell research is the sourcing of embryonic stem cells that may be used in such research. The law and policy related to the population control policy have the potential to create an abundance of embryonic bodies for stem cell research.

As discussed above, the Guidelines allow unwanted gametes or blastulas from IVF procedures, embryo cells from miscarriages or voluntarily induced abortions, and donated germ cells to be used in human embryonic stem cell research.[33] The population control policy has resulted in a high abortion rate. With the written consent of the donor and following review by the ethics committee, embryo cells from abortions may be used in stem cell research.[34]

Furthermore, due to the "one-child policy," couples who have had successful IVF are in most cases unable to use their leftover embryos for the conception of more children. The ART Ethical Principles allow unused embryos to be used for stem cell research, with the written consent of patients. Although couples may decide how to dispose of the leftover IVF gametes and embryos, the ART Ethical Principles prohibit medical personnel from performing assisted pregnancy with donated embryos, which seems to have barred the donation of the leftover IVF embryos to other childless couples.[35] If so, there are only two remaining options to deal with the embryos: discard them as waste or give consent for donation of the embryos to scientific research.[36]

[2003] No. 176, June 27, 2003), http://www.moh.gov.cn/publicfiles/business/htmlfiles/mohkjjys/s3581/200805/35747.htm (in Chinese).

[28] ART Order art. 3.

[29] *Id.* art. 22.

[30] *Id.* arts. 6, 14.

[31] *Id.* art. 14.

[32] *Id.* art. 19.

[33] Guidelines for Ethical Principles in Human Embryonic Stem Cell Research, *supra* note 4, art. 5.

[34] *Id.* arts. 8 & 9.

[35] Ethical Principles §§ 1.1.3 & 1.3.6., *supra* note 27. *See also* Klein, *supra* note 12, at 412.

[36] Klein, *supra* note 12, at 413.

In recent years, China has also issued a couple of rules and regulations in other biomedical fields, including research on human subjects and organ transplantation, which are currently subject to ethics review.[37]

IV. Concluding Remarks

Some have suggested that China's unrestrictive regulatory regime of biomedical research, as well that of abortion, is due to a different cultural view toward life. According to that accepted cultural view, they reason, a person comes into existence at birth, and a human embryo should not be treated morally as a person or life. Therefore, destroying an embryo during biomedical research or an abortion should not be viewed as killing a person.[38] Even if this is a commonly accepted viewpoint, it is unclear to what extent the public's cultural views can affect the regulatory regime in China. As shown in this report, such regulations may be shaped by the government's attitude and its political needs—in particular, the promotion of scientific advancement and population control—rather than by public opinion.

Prepared by Laney Zhang
Senior Foreign Law Specialist
September 2012

---

[37] *See, e.g.* Sheji Ren de Shengwu Yixue Yanjiu Lunli [Regulations on Ethical Review of Biomedical Research Involving Human Subject (Trial)] (Wei Ke Jiao Fa [2007] No. 17, issued by the MOH on Jan. 11, 2007), art. 1, http://www.moh.gov.cn/publicfiles/business/htmlfiles/ mohkjjys/s3581/200804/18816 htm (in Chinese). Renti Qiguan Yizhi Tiaoli [The Regulations on Human Organ Transplantation] (promulgated by the State Council on Mar. 31, 2007, effective May 1, 2007), art. 15, 15 STATE COUNCIL GAZ. 2007 at 12–15 (in Chinese).

[38] Wang Yuangunag, *Chinese Ethical Views on Embryo Stem (ES) Cell Research, in* EUBIOS ETHICS INSTITUTE, ASIAN BIOETHICS IN THE 21ST CENTURY, http://www.eubios.info/ABC4/abc4049 htm (last visited Sept. 10, 2012).

LAW LIBRARY OF CONGRESS

ISRAEL

REGULATION OF SURROGACY BIRTH: ETHICAL CONSIDERATIONS

Executive Summary

Surrogacy conducted in Israel is regulated by the Agreements for the Carriage of Fetuses (Approval of Agreement and Status of the Newborn) Law, 5756-1996. The Law requires surrogacy agreements to be approved by a committee that evaluates various conditions, including psychological and social conditions, regarding both the surrogate and the parents. Scholars, as well as a public committee appointed by the Minister of Health in 2010, have reviewed the legal and ethical considerations surrounding surrogacy, and made recommendations in view of the experience gained in this area since the enactment of the Law in 1996.

I. Background

Modern reproductive technologies, such as in vitro fertilization (IVF) and the use of assisted reproductive technology (ART), along with a pro-natalist state policy of fully or partially subsidizing such treatments, have made it possible for an increased number of Israeli women, including unmarried or infertile women and those wishing to delay procreation to facilitate career development, to give birth.[1] ART has also facilitated pregnancies by surrogate mothers, thereby enabling men and women to obtain babies that were conceived by IVF, whether or not by using their own genetic material.

Surrogacy motherhood was first regulated by law in Israel on March 17, 1996, when the Knesset (Parliament) passed the Agreements for the Carriage of Fetuses (Approval of Agreement and Status of the Newborn) Law, 5756-1996[2] (hereafter the Surrogacy Agreements Law). This Law regulates surrogacy agreements that are conducted in Israel (intrastate surrogacy) but does not address surrogacy involving foreign surrogates (interstate surrogacy).

According to data provided in 2012 to the Knesset Information and Research Center (KIRC) by Israel's Ministry of Health, the number of requests for approval of surrogacy agreements under the Surrogacy Agreements Law, and as a consequence, the number of babies

---

[1] For further information, *see* RUTH LEVUSH, ISRAEL: REPRODUCTION AND ABORTION: LAW AND POLICY, (Law Library of Congress, 2012), http://www.loc.gov/law/help/israel_reproduction_law_policy.php.

[2] Agreements for the Carriage of Fetuses (Approval of Agreement and Status of the Newborn) Law, 5756-1996 (hereafter Surrogacy Agreements Law), SH No. 1577, p. 176.

born through domestic surrogacy, has been steadily on the rise.[3] The increase in the number of requests filed with Israeli family courts for genetic testing and a determination of legal status in cases involving interstate surrogacy has similarly been viewed as an indication of a rise in the number of babies born in interstate surrogacy.[4]

Numerous ethical concerns were raised in Israel in connection with both intrastate and interstate surrogacy procedures. In June 2010 the Ministry of Health established the Public Committee for Evaluation of the Legislative Regulation of the Subject of Fertility and Giving Birth in Israel[5] (hereafter the Public Committee on Fertility). The Committee published its recommendations in May 2012.[6] Among its recommendations, the Committee proposed several changes to current law regarding intrastate and interstate surrogacy.[7]

II. The Committee for Approval of Surrogacy Agreements

Intrastate surrogacy agreements must currently be approved by the Committee for Approval. The Committee is appointed by the Minister of Health based on authorization provided by the Surrogacy Agreements Law. The Committee, which sits behind closed doors, includes the following seven members:

1. Two doctors who hold the title of experts in obstetrics and gynecology

2. A doctor who holds the title of an expert in internal medicine

3. A clinical psychologist

4. A social worker

5. A public representative who is a lawyer

6. A religious representative, according to the religion of the parties to the surrogacy agreement[8]

---

[3] ORLY ALMAGOR LOTAN, SURROGACY IN ISRAEL AND SURROGACY OF ISRAELIS ABROAD: THE CURRENT SITUATION AND PRESENTATION OF PUBLIC COMMITTEE FOR ITS CHANGE 5 (Knesset Information and Research Center (KIRC, May 29, 2012), http://www.knesset.gov.il/mmm/data/pdf/m03065.pdf (in Hebrew).

[4] *Id.* at 11.

[5] *Public Committee for Evaluation of the Legislative Regulation of the Subject of Fertility and Giving Birth in Israel*, MINISTRY OF HEALTH, http://www.old health.gov.il/pages/default.asp?maincat=1&catid=6&pageid=5171 (in Hebrew; last visited June 12, 2012).

[6] RECOMMENDATIONS OF THE PUBLIC COMMITTEE FOR EVALUATION OF THE LEGISLATIVE REGULATION OF THE SUBJECT OF FERTILITY AND GIVING BIRTH IN ISRAEL (Avital Viner-Oman ed., May 2012), http://www.health.gov.il/PublicationsFiles/BAP2012.pdf (in Hebrew).

[7] *Id.* at 65, 67–68.

[8] Surrogacy Agreements Law § 3, SH No. 1577, p. 176.

III. Conditions for Approval of Surrogacy Agreements

The Surrogacy Agreements Law restricts eligibility for surrogacy agreements to couples who contract with a surrogate to bear a child due to medical reasons that prevent the woman from completing a pregnancy.

The Law generally requires a surrogate to be unmarried and to not be a relative of any of the designated parents; the semen used for the IVF to be from the designated father and the ova not to be from the surrogate; and the surrogate to belong to the same religion as the designated mother, except upon the opinion of a religious official where all parties are not Jewish.[9]

A request for approval of a surrogacy agreement must be accompanied by the agreement, a medical opinion regarding the inability of the designated mother to bear a child, a medical and psychological evaluation regarding the suitability of each one of the parties to engage in surrogacy, a confirmation by a psychologist or a social worker that the designated parents received suitable professional consultation including information on other parenting opportunities, and information regarding any agency that was involved in procuring the agreement.[10]

The Committee for Approval will approve the agreement after verifying that all the above documents were submitted; that all parties entered the agreement upon their own free will, having understood its meaning and potential consequences; and that the agreement does not pose a threat to the health of the surrogate mother or the expected child, or the rights of any of the parties.[11]

IV. Legal Challenges to the Current Law

Two lawsuits have been filed targeting the restricted application of the Surrogacy Agreements Law to heterosexual married couples. The first involved a petition by a single woman who underwent surgery to remove her uterus. She requested authorization for the implantation of her fertilized ova, extracted before her surgery, in a surrogate.

In his 2002 decision, Justice Michael Cheshin recognized that the Surrogacy Agreements Law applied differential treatment in preventing single women from contracting with surrogates to bear their child. He determined, however, that the differential treatment under the Law at that time was proportional, and therefore legal, due to the experimental nature of the Law and the limited experience gained since its passage. Other justices consented but recommended that the legislature review the appropriateness of the Law, including its differential treatment of single women, based on the experience that had been gained since its enactment.[12]

---

[9] *Id.*

[10] *Id.* § 4.

[11] *Id.* § 5.

[12] H.C. 2458/01 New Family v. the Committee for Approval of Surrogacy Agreements, 54 PISKE DIN [PD] [DECISIONS OF THE SUPREME COURT] 419 (2003).

A second petition against the alleged discriminatory application of the Law was filed by a gay couple and quashed by consent in view of the establishment of the Public Committee on Fertility.[13]

V. Ethical Considerations Associated with Surrogacy Agreements

The Public Committee on Fertility evaluated several ethical considerations relating to the legal status and rights of surrogate mothers. Specifically, the Committee pondered whether surrogacy procedures were legitimate because of the surrogate's autonomy over her body and her ongoing authority to make decisions regarding its use. The Committee further reflected on whether "no payment should be made for the use of one person's organs for the benefit of another, because it is necessary to protect women who, for economic or other considerations might enter a potentially risky procedure or at least [one that] involves some pain and suffering, and all to provide a solution to a medical problem of other people."[14]

The Public Committee on Fertility recognized the physical and emotional impact of surrogacy on surrogates. Referring to the findings in a report by Israeli scholars Nofar Lipkin and Eti Samama,[15] the Committee listed the following impacts of surrogacy:

A. Physical Impact on Surrogates

Surrogacy exposes the surrogate to hormonal treatment prior to implantation; to pregnancy risks, particularly those associated with multiple embryos; to risks associated with delivery, including a high level of c-sections; and to additional long-term health risks that are linked to repeated hormonal treatment cycles (on average 2.5 treatment cycles, but in some cases up to seven) that have been found to be required for a successful implantation that results in the delivery of a child.[16]

B. Emotional Impact on Surrogates

The knowledge that the child carried by the surrogate would be delivered to others after birth was found to have made surrogates attempt to unnaturally detach emotionally from the fetus they were carrying. Additionally, surrogates were often found to have developed emotional dependency on the prospective parents, resulting in deep disappointment, and sometimes trauma, after the delivery, when the parents detached themselves from the surrogate. Surrogates were also found to have significantly lost their privacy throughout the procedure both by having to undergo treatments and take medications during pregnancy not upon their own discretion, and by

---

[13] H.C. 1078/10 Pinkas v. the Committee for Approval of Surrogacy Agreements [2010], available on the Nevo Legal Database *at* http://www.nevo.co.il (by subscription; last visited June 13, 2012).

[14] RECOMMENDATIONS OF THE PUBLIC COMMITTEE, *supra* note 6, at 51 (translated by author, R.L.).

[15] NOFAR LIPKIN & ETI SAMAMA, SURROGACY IN ISRAEL: STATUS VIEW 2010 AND PROPOSALS FOR LEGISLATIVE AMENDMENTS (Isha LeIsha [Woman to Woman], Haifa, 2011), http://www.isha.org.il/upload/file/%D7%90%D7%99%D7%A0%D7%93%D7%A7%D7%A1/surrogacy_web.pdf (last visited Aug. 6, 2012).

[16] RECOMMENDATIONS OF THE PUBLIC COMMITTEE, *supra* note 6, at 58.

having to abide by other requirements made by the prospective parents. Such requirements were often found to include such things as a prohibition on smoking, a prohibition on traveling abroad, eating kosher food, and refraining from sexual intercourse.[17]

C. Impact on Surrogates' Other Children

Interviews conducted with surrogates indicated distress on the part of their own children, who viewed the transfer of the baby carried by their mother to the couple who engaged the surrogate as the loss of a family member, and expressed fear that they, like the baby, might be given to other parents. The need for some surrogates to stay on bed rest for long periods during pregnancy was also found to have a lasting impact on their children, who, considering the requirement that the surrogate not be married, have either experienced divorce or have never had a father, according to the report.[18]

D. Interstate Surrogacy Agreements

The Public Committee on Fertility also addressed the legal and ethical considerations specifically associated with interstate surrogacy agreements. Such agreements first involved Israeli gay couples, and were later extended to Israeli married couples who, for reasons including a possible shortage of Israeli surrogate mothers, economics, a wish to speed up the required approval procedures, or an effort to sever connections between parents and the surrogate, have decided to engage in interstate surrogacy agreements.[19]

Interstate surrogacy was found to pose challenges for couples and individuals who wish to enter Israel with a child that was born abroad. Among relevant considerations are those related to proof of genetic relations, ensuring that the child has not been kidnapped from the country where he was born, that the case did not involve trade in babies without any genetic connection to the Israeli parent, an evaluation of the legality of the procedure in the country in which it was performed, etc.[20]

VI. Concluding Remarks

In its report the Public Committee on Fertility proposed that approval of surrogacy should extend to childless unmarried women who cannot bear a pregnancy for medical reasons, to single men, and to married couples who do not have more than one child together. Unlike for single women, surrogacy can be approved for single men for altruistic reasons only, to prevent competition and the rising prices for surrogacy services.[21] In order to increase the number of potential surrogates the Committee also recommended eliminating the current prohibition on married women and certain types of relatives serving as surrogates.

---

[17] *Id.* at 58–59.

[18] *Id.* at 59.

[19] *Id.* at 66.

[20] *Id.* at 68.

[21] *Id.* at 16.

To protect the surrogate mother the Committee recommended limiting the number of implantation cycles a surrogate can undergo to three, and to two babies only in each cycle; requiring the inclusion of a health care provision in the surrogacy agreement as a condition for its approval; and, to avoid a conflict of interest, requiring a separation between the medical team that cares for the surrogate and the team that cares for the designated mother. The Committee further recommended supervising corporations and organizations that act as intermediates in surrogacy arrangements for a fee.[22]

To address the concerns raised regarding interstate surrogacy, the Committee also recommended the adoption of a procedure for approval by a bi-ministerial committee. Such approval would require compliance with both medical and legal requirements, such as proof of the foreign surrogate's informed consent as well as of the foreign law's recognition of the surrogacy. An approval of interstate surrogacy, according to the Committee, should result in facilitation of receipt of a decree recognizing parenthood without the need to go through adoption proceedings, as is currently necessary. Such approval would also result in eligibility for public funding for ova fertilization if it is done in Israel, similar to that available in cases involving intrastate surrogacy.[23]

Recognizing the potential conflict of laws regarding the identity and the citizenship of parents and the implications for the status of the surrogates in cases involving interstate surrogacy, the Committee called for cooperation among countries and for the adoption of an international treaty that will regulate interstate surrogacy and provide for appropriate standards for implementation.[24]

Nofar Lipkin and Eti Samama, whose comprehensive study on surrogacy in Israel was heavily cited by the Committee, have expressed major concerns regarding the potential impact of increasing surrogacy in Israel on current social norms, particularly on diminishing the importance of the connection between the mother and the fetus she is carrying.[25] Such social developments, they argued, pose significant dangers both to surrogate mothers and to Israeli society as a whole.[26]

Prepared by Ruth Levush
Senior Foreign Law Specialist
July 2012

---

[22] *Id.* at 65.

[23] *Id.* at 68-89.

[24] *Id.* at 68.

[25] LIPKIN & SAMAMA, *supra* note 15, at 17.

[26] *Id.*

LAW LIBRARY OF CONGRESS

INDIA

REGULATION OF SURROGACY AND FERTILITY CLINICS

Executive Summary

India has become the top destination in the world for commercial surrogacy, primarily due to low costs and almost nonexistent regulations. Although the Ministry of Health and Family Welfare and the Indian Council of Medical Research (ICMR), India's main body for advancing biomedical research, have issued nonbinding National Guidelines, comprehensive legislation regulating surrogacy and assisted reproductive technology (ART) clinics is yet to be enacted. However, draft legislation—the Assisted Reproductive Technologies (Regulation) Bill—is expected to be presented to Parliament during the winter session this year and is expected to pass.

The current lack of regulations has raised a number of ethical and legal concerns, particularly regarding the exploitation and abuse of surrogate mothers. The status and rights of the commissioning parent(s) as well as of the children are of equally deep concern.

I. Introduction

Surrogacy is a fast-growing but unregulated industry in India that, according to an earlier Confederation of Indian Industry estimate, was expected to generate as much as $2.3 billion annually by 2012.[1] A Kennan Institute of Ethics case study suggests that "fertility tourism" in India and other developing countries emerged in response to greater regulation and stricter laws in industrialized countries.[2] The key reasons India became the "world's top destination for commercial surrogacy" include "lower costs" and the total absence of government regulations or laws.[3] Though there is no exact data, some news reports claim there are "about 500 fertility

---

[1] Divya Gupta, *Inside India's Surrogacy Industry*, THE GUARDIAN (Dec. 6, 2011), http://www.guardian .co.uk/world/2011/dec/06/surrogate-mothers-india (citing Confederation of Indian Industry report).

[2] Kari Points, *Commercial Surrogacy and Fertility Tourism in India: The Case of Baby Manji*, CASE STUDIES IN ETHICS (Kennan Institute for Ethics, Duke University, 2009), at 3, http://www.duke.edu/web/ kenanethics/CaseStudies/BabyManji.pdf.

[3] *Id.*

treatment clinics across the country."[4] Other news reports indicate that there may be as many as 1,000 fertility and surrogacy clinics in the country.[5]

According to critics and activists, the lack of a legal framework and the increasing commercialization of the industry have "left room for unethical medical practices and the exploitation of both surrogates and infertile couples."[6]

II. Legal and Administrative Framework

Various sources refer to surrogacy being legalized in India in 2002,[7] when draft guidelines were first issued by the Indian Council of Medical Research (ICMR).[8] The nonbinding guidelines were then updated and finalized in 2005. In 2008, in the Baby Manji case, the Supreme Court of India recognized that commercial surrogacy is legal in India and was reaching "industry proportions" due to "high international demand and ready availability of poor surrogates."[9] As at the time of this report, however, there is still no federal law regulating the industry, although draft legislation is under consideration.

A. National Guidelines

The Ministry of Health and Family Welfare and the Indian Council of Medical Research (ICMR), India's "apex body" for the "formulation, coordination and promotion of biomedical research,"[10] issued National Guidelines for Accreditation, Supervision and Regulation of ART (Assisted Reproductive Technology) Clinics in India in 2005.[11] Although the National Guidelines were intended "to ensure that ART clinics in India are accredited, regulated and supervised,"[12] they have had little impact on regulating the industry because they are not legally binding.[13] Apart from providing guidance on "matters relating to the accreditation, supervision,

---

[4] Swati Deshpande, *Time for Law on Assisted Fertility Technology, Experts Say*, TIMES OF INDIA (July 13, 2012), http://articles.timesofindia.indiatimes.com/2012-07-13/mumbai/32662675_1_egg-donor-egg-donation-new-law.

[5] Shekhar Bhatia, *Revealed: How More and More Britons are Paying Indian Women to Become Surrogate Mothers,* THE TELEGRAPH (May 26, 2012), http://www.telegraph.co.uk/health/healthnews/9292343/Revealed-how-more-and-more-Britons-are-paying-Indian-women-to-become-surrogate-mothers.html.

[6] Gupta, *supra* note 1.

[7] *See, e.g.,* Mina Chang, *Womb for Rent*, HARVARD INTERNATIONAL REVIEW (July 6, 2009), http://hir.harvard.edu/frontiers-of-conflict/womb-for-rent.

[8] Points, *supra* note 2, at 3.

[9] Baby Manji Yamada v. Union of India & Anr. (2008) I.N.S.C. 1656, *available at* http://www.liiofindia.org/in/cases/cen/INSC/2008/1656.html.

[10] *About Us*, INDIAN COUNCIL OF MEDICAL RESEARCH (ICMR), http://www.icmr.nic.in/About_Us/About_Us.html (last visited Aug. 30, 2012).

[11] MINISTRY OF HEALTH AND FAMILY WELFARE & ICMR, NATIONAL ACADEMY OF MEDICAL SCIENCES [hereinafter MINISTRY OF HEALTH & ICMR], NATIONAL GUIDELINES FOR ACCREDITATION, SUPERVISION AND REGULATION OF ART CLINICS IN INDIA (2005), http://icmr.nic.in/art/art_clinics.htm.

[12] *Id.* at 4.

[13] Points, *supra* note 2, at 3.

and regulation of ART clinics,"[14] the document includes provisions on gamete transfers, surrogacy, and parental rights.[15]

As guiding rules and principles, the Guidelines have been heavily criticized for "reinforcing social prejudice"[16] regarding infertility and treating certain crucial issues, such as informed consent, "rather summarily and in vague terms."[17] In general, critics state that the Guidelines do not do enough to protect surrogate mothers from abuse or exploitation.[18]

B. Assisted Reproductive Technologies (Regulation) Bill

Proposed legislation to regulate India's assisted reproductive industry, the Assisted Reproductive Technology (Regulation) Bill (the Draft Bill),[19] will be taken up by Parliament in the winter of 2012 and is expected to pass. The need for regulating commercial surrogacy was highlighted in a 2009 report by the Law Commission of India, which stated that "[t]he legal issues related with surrogacy, as we have seen, are very complex and need to be addressed by a comprehensive legislation"[20] The legislative initiative received additional impetus after a 2010 incident in which a seventeen-year-old girl, Sushma Pandey, died "two days after her last egg donation."[21]

Currently, any person can open an ART clinic and no authorization is required. Under the Draft Bill all ART clinics would be required to register with a Registration Authority.[22] Registration would only be approved, through the issuance of a registration number, once the clinic met minimum requirements set by the ICMR.[23] The Bill would also establish a National Advisory Board and State Boards to monitor ART clinics.[24]

The Bill contains rules on "sourcing, storage, handling and record keeping for gametes, embryos and surrogates,"[25] and seeks to regulate "research on embryos, gametes or other human

---

[14] Usha Rengachary Smerdon, *Crossing Bodies, Crossing Borders: International Surrogacy Between the United States and India*, 39 CUMB. L. REV. 15, 35 (2008–2009).

[15] *Id.*

[16] Siddhartha Chatterjee & Rajib Gon Chowdhury, *Third Party Reproduction in Recent Scenario*, 105 J. INDIAN MED. ASSOC. 242 (2007), *available at* http://www.issuesinmedicalethics.org/153cm123.html.

[17] *Id.*

[18] *Id.*

[19] The Assisted Reproductive Technologies (Regulation) Bill, 2010 (Draft), *available at* http://www.icmr.nic.in/guide/ART%20REGULATION%20Draft%20Bill1.pdf.

[20] LAW COMMISSION OF INDIA, NEED FOR LEGISLATION TO REGULATE ASSISTED REPRODUCTIVE TECHNOLOGY CLINICS AS WELL AS RIGHTS AND OBLIGATIONS OF PARTIES TO A SURROGACY, Rep. No. 228, ¶ 2.1 (Aug. 5, 2009), http://lawcommissionofindia.nic.in/reports/report228.pdf.

[21] Deshpande, *supra* note 4.

[22] The Assisted Reproductive Technologies (Regulation) Bill § 13.

[23] *Id.* § 15

[24] *Id.* §§ 3–12.

[25] *Id.* ch. V.

reproductive material."[26] In addition, it spells out some of the rights and duties of donors, patients, surrogates, and children.[27] The Bill would introduce several other significant provisions: any woman who is "less than twenty one years of age and over thirty five years of age [would not] be eligible to act as a surrogate mother,"[28] and "no woman [could] act as a surrogate for more than five successful live births in her life, including her own children."[29] However, as noted by Sama, an Indian women's health organization, the Bill does not "address the number of assisted reproductive cycles a woman can experience."[30]

The Bill would also allow surrogacy through in vitro fertilization (IVF) and embryo transfer (ET), but prohibit genetic surrogacy through intrauterine insemination (IUI).[31] In addition, it would prohibit foreigners whose home countries do not permit surrogacy from using surrogacy services in India.[32] Notably, the Bill would grant all parentage rights to the commissioning parent(s).[33] Under the Bill, a foreign commissioning parent(s) or "a non-resident Indian individual or couple" seeking surrogacy in India would be required to appoint a local guardian who would be "legally responsible for taking care of the surrogate during and after the pregnancy . . . , till the child / children are delivered to the foreigner or foreign couple or the local guardian."[34]

The Bill was prepared and published by the ICMR in conjunction with the Ministry of Health and Family Welfare. It has been sent to the Ministry of Law for approval and is expected to be introduced during the winter session of Parliament.[35] While the Bill is being finalized, the Ministry of Health and Family Welfare and ICMR have begun the process of setting up the National Registry of Assisted Reproductive Technology,[36] which will act as the Registration Authority referenced in the Bill.

---

[26] *Id.* ch. VI.

[27] *Id.* ch. VII.

[28] *Id.* § 34(5).

[29] *Id.*

[30] Nilanjana S. Roy, *Protecting the Rights of Surrogate Mothers in India*, NEW YORK TIMES (Oct. 4, 2011), http://www.nytimes.com/2011/10/05/world/asia/05iht-letter05.html; *see also* Letter from Sama Resource Group for Women and Health to Dr. A Ramadoss, Union Minister for Health and Family Welfare (Dec. 4, 2008), http://www.samawomenshealth.org/downloads/ART%20Bill%20Critique_Sama.pdf; *The Regulation of Surrogacy in India: Questions and Complexities,* SAMA· RESOURCE GROUP FOR WOMEN AND HEALTH (Apr. 23, 2011), http://samawomenshealth.wordpress.com/2011/04/23/the-regulation-of-surrogacy-in-india-questions-and-complexities/.

[31] *The Regulation of Surrogacy in India, supra* note 30.

[32] The Assisted Reproductive Technologies (Regulation) Bill § 34(19).

[33] *Id.* § 35.

[34] *Id.* § 34(19).

[35] Deshpande, *supra* note 4.

[36] *National Registry of ART Clinics in India*, ICMR, http://www.icmr.nic.in/icmrnews/National_Registry_ART.pdf (last visited Sept. 10, 2012).

III. Ethical Concerns

Recently, legal scholars and ethicists have raised a number of ethical, social, and legal concerns with respect to the surrogacy industry in India.

Some critics have questioned the notion of free choice or free will, because most Indian women who agree to surrogacy arrangements do so due to dire circumstances.[37] Professor Raywat Deonandan, an expert on the global industry of reproductive medical tourism, commenting on the problem of exploitation, states that,

> [w]hen clients from a wealthy country such as the United States, Canada, or the United Kingdom seek biological services from vulnerable—and likely uneducated—individuals in a poor country like India, the opportunity for exploitation, even unintentional, is great. A maternal surrogate in India is handsomely paid, receiving anything from $2,000 to $8,000 per pregnancy, which is considerably more than she is typically likely to see in a year. A strictly libertarian argument holds that "fair" monetary compensation, combined with freedom of choice, obviates any ethical concern. A more nuanced perspective asks, if the alternative is poverty and death, is there really a choice at all? This is the classic tension between autonomy and exploitation, in that a desperately poor person can be co-opted to express her autonomy in such a way that it leads to her exploitation.[38]

According to another scholar, Usha Rengachary Smerdon, "[f]ree choice must also be questioned in terms of what is meant by informed consent and the extent to which surrogates are adequately counseled about the physical risks of surrogacy."[39]

Critics also note the risk of exploitation by surrogacy clinics that may have more financial incentives to look out for the interests of the client rather than the surrogate. According to Deonandan, "from a medical perspective, the clinician is directly responsible for the care of both the client and the surrogate,"[40] clearly creating a conflict of interest. Deonandan notes that "[t]he absence of an independent medical advocate acting on behalf of the surrogate immediately nudges this relationship into the realm of exploitation."[41] Commissioning couples may also be "lured into surrogacy through other unethical practices,"[42] including false or misleading advertising.

Commenting on the social stigma associated with surrogacy, Smerdon adds that "traditional Indian attitudes towards sex and procreation often force a surrogate to hide her

---

[37] Smerdon, *supra* note 14, at 54.

[38] Raywat Deonandan, *The Ethics of Surrogacy*, INDIA CURRENTS (Feb. 3, 2012), http://www.indiacurrents. com/articles/2012/02/03/ethics-surrogacy.

[39] Smerdon, *supra* note 14, at 54

[40] Deonandan, supra note 38.

[41] *Id.*

[42] *Id.* at 57.

pregnancy and/or invent stories about her pregnancy—for example, saying the baby has died or that they have been away for months on the pretext of visiting relatives."[43]

In addition to these concerns, critics have also commented on the unclear legal status of children born through surrogacy in India, "thereby threatening their future economic, familial, and legal security,"[44] and on the psychological costs for both the surrogate mother and commissioning parent(s) during and after the pregnancy.[45] These and other concerns have led many critics to call for comprehensive legislation regulating the surrogacy industry in India, as is being currently considered with the ART Bill.

Prepared by Tariq Ahmad
Legal Research Analyst
September 2012

---

[43] Smerdon, *supra* note 14, at 56

[44] *Id.* at 62.

[45] *Id.* at 56.

LAW LIBRARY OF CONGRESS

KENYA

REGULATION OF GENETICALLY MODIFIED ORGANISMS

Executive Summary

Kenya recently introduced a robust regulatory regime to govern the development, release, and commercialization of genetically modified organisms (GMOs). The regime is designed to promote advancements in biotechnology to, among other aims, modernize the agricultural sector and ensure food security while minimizing the risks to human health and the environment associated with GMO-related activities. The regime does this by establishing specific rules and procedures for conducting GMO-related activities (including regulations on contained use; environmental release; import, export, and transit; and commercialization) and a regulatory body with a mandate to process applications for such activities and monitor compliance with the relevant laws and regulations.

I. Background

Kenya's biosafety regulatory framework includes the 2006 National Biotechnology Development Policy[1] and the Biosafety Act of 2009[2] and subsidiary legislation—the Environmental Release Regulations; Import, Export and Transit Regulations; Contained Use Regulations; and Labeling Regulations.[3]

Two competing themes are evident throughout this regulatory regime. The first is the recognition that Kenya needs to exploit advancements made in biotechnology, particularly in the field of agriculture. The Policy makes this clear:

[T]he [Kenyan] government has certainly identified biotechnology as an appropriate tool and vehicle that can deliver economic gains through intellectual property creation to

---

[1] REPUBLIC OF KENYA, A NATIONAL BIOTECHNOLOGY DEVELOPMENT POLICY (2006), *available at* http://en.biosafetyscanner.org/pdf/doc/350_allegato.pdf (Genetic Rights Foundation website).

[2] The Biosafety Act, No. 2 (2009), KENYA GAZETTE SUPPLEMENT No. 10 (Feb. 13, 2009), *available at* http://www.biosafetykenya.go.ke/index.php?option=com_docman&task=doc_download&gid=43&Itemid=471.

[3] The Biosafety (Environmental Release) Regulations, 2011 (July 15, 2011), § 10; the Biosafety (Import, Export and Transit) Regulations, 2011 (July 15, 2011), §§ 4, 6–7; the Biosafety (Contained Use) Regulations, 2011 (July 15, 2011), § 5; *and* the Biosafety (Labeling) Regulations, 2012 (May 7, 2012), § 3, all four *available at* Kenya Law Reports (KLR) website, http://www.kenyalaw.org/kenyalaw/klr_home/index.php (in the Act Title tab, scroll down to Biosafety Act, click Search, and then scroll down to the text of the relevant regulation).

expand entrepreneurial opportunities for industrial growth, reduction of poverty, and improvement of food security, health, and environmental sustainability.[4]

This theme recurred throughout the legislative debates on the Biosafety Bill, in which various lawmakers and government representatives advocated for its enactment so that genetically modified organisms (GMOs) that had been in controlled trials could be commercialized and additional trials could be performed.[5]

The second theme is an acknowledgment of the possible negative ramifications that come with the development and application of biotechnology. As discussed below, this is evident in the language and tone of the Biosafety Act and its subsidiary legislation. The regulatory regime seeks to reconcile the two themes by encouraging the development, commercialization, and use of GMOs while, at the same time, putting in place comprehensive legal and institutional mechanisms to ensure the safety of human health and the environment.

Kenyan scientists have been engaging in biotechnology activities, particularly in the agriculture sector, for over two decades. The first attempt in this field was in 1991, when a genetically modified virus-resistant sweet potato was developed,[6] followed by various contained field trials of other types of crops, including insect-resistant (Bt) maize, insect-resistant cotton, and virus-resistant cassava.[7] However, none of these genetically modified crops were approved for environmental release or commercial availability,[8] in large part because Kenya lacked the legal framework for doing so.[9]

The provisional regulatory framework in place prior to enactment of the Biosafety Act had various problems. A major impediment was the fact that it operated in a "legislative vacuum,"[10] in the absence of any parliamentary action. The provisional regulatory regime only came into being in 1998, seven years after Kenya first began experimenting with genetically modified crops, when the National Council for Science and Technology (NCST) issued

---

[4] REPUBLIC OF KENYA, *supra* note 1, at 5.

[5] KENYA NATIONAL ASSEMBLY OFFICIAL REPORT (HANSARD) (Dec. 2, 2008), 3755–81, *available to download at* http://www.parliament.go.ke/index.php?option=com_docman&task=doc_download&gid=844&Itemid=; HANSARD (Oct. 2, 2007), 4282–84, *available to download at* http://www.parliament.go.ke/index.php?option=com_docman&task=doc_details&gid=1033&Itemid=; M. KAREMBU ET AL., DEVELOPING A BIOSAFETY LAW: LESSONS FROM THE KENYAN EXPERIENCE 17–27 (International Service for the Acquisition of Agri-Biotech Applications, 2010), http://www.isaaa.org/resources/publications/developing_a_biosafety_law-lessons_from_the_kenya n_experience/download/Developing%20a%20Biosafety%20Law%20-%20Lessons%20from%20the%20 Kenyan%20Experience.pdf.

[6] Matthew Harsh, *Formal and Informal Governance of Agricultural Biotechnology in Kenya: Participation and Accountability in Controversy Surrounding the Draft Biosafety Bill*, 17 J. INT. DEV. 661, 662 (2005).

[7] *Id.* at 663; *Approved Confined Field Trials (CFTs) Activities of Genetically Modified Organisms*, BIOSAFETY CLEARING-HOUSE KENYA, http://ke.biosafetyclearinghouse net/approvedcft.shtml (last visited Aug. 30, 2012).

[8] Roy B. Mugiira, *Administrative Systems for Handling Biosafety Issues in Kenya*, 9 BIOSAFETY PROTOCOL NEWS 10, 11 (July 2011), *available at* https://bch.cbd.int/protocol /outreach/newsletter/bpn-09.pdf.

[9] KAREMBU ET AL., *supra* note 5, at 5.

[10] Harsh, *supra* note 6, at 669.

Regulations and Guidelines for Biosafety in Biotechnology under the Science and Technology Act.[11] The NCST established the National Biosafety Committee (NBC) to develop a biosafety policy for Kenya and review applications for GMO-related activities.[12] However, the Science and Technology Act did not give the NCST any regulatory mandate[13] and, therefore, the NBC lacked enforcement and compliance authority.[14] Once the NBC approved controlled field trials of various crops, it lacked the mandate to approve wider trials, the release of GMOs into the environment, and product commercialization. The legislative vacuum resulted in a fragmented, inefficient regulatory environment in which multiple government institutions attempted to regulate matters pertaining to biosafety, with no one institution having coordinating authority.[15]

The process to modernize the regulatory framework, which began in the early 2000s, took over a decade to complete. Kenya signed the 2000 Cartagena Protocol on Biosafety, which came into force on September 11, 2003, and was ratified by Kenya that same year.[16] Kenya was therefore obligated to put in place a regulatory mechanism to implement the Protocol.[17] However, a Biosafety Bill proposed in 2002 could not progress in Parliament for a number of reasons. The Bill encountered opposition from various civil society organizations.[18] The process of "reconciling diverse interests of stakeholders" as well as the lawmakers' lack of fluency in biotechnology issues also slowed down the Bill's progress.[19] Furthermore, the Bill became a casualty of political changes in Kenya, when election cycles resulted in the ouster of key players in Parliament and the executive branch, who had worked on and arrived at a good understanding of the issues at hand.[20] In 2006, while the Bill was still languishing in Parliament,

---

[11] *See* Gregory Jaffe, *Comparative Analysis of the National Biosafety Regulatory Systems in East Africa* 17 (International Food Policy Research Institute, Environment and Production Technology Division, EPT Discussion Paper 146, Jan. 2006), http://www.ifpri.org/sites/default/files/publications/eptdp146.pdf; Science and Technology Act of 1977, Cap. 250 (rev. ed. 2009), *available at* KLR, http://www.kenyalaw.org/Downloads/Acts/SCIENCE%20 AND%20TECHNOLOGY%20ACT%28Cap.%20250%29.pdf.

[12] *Status of Biotechnology in Kenya*, AFRICAN BIOTECHNOLOGY, http://www.absfafrica.org/index.php?optio n=com_content&view=article&id=36&Itemid=11 (last visited Aug. 29, 2012).

[13] Harsh, *supra* note 6, at 669.

[14] *Id.*; Jaffe, *supra* note 11, at 17.

[15] Harsh, *supra* note 6, at 669.

[16] Cartagena Protocol on Biosafety to the Convention on Biological Diversity, Jan. 29, 2000, http://bch.cbd.int/protocol/text/; *see also* KAREMBU ET AL., *supra* note 5, at 4.

[17] Ann Njoki Kingiri, *The Contested Framing of Biosafety Regulation as a Tool for Enhancing Public Awareness: Insights from the Kenyan Regulatory Process and bioAWARE Strategy*, 2(1) INT. J. TECH. & DEV. STUD. 64, 70 (2011), http://www.ijtds.com/IJTDS2_3_kingiri.pdf.

[18] David Njagi & Christina Scott, *Kenya Prepares to Approve Biosafety Legislation*, SCIDEV.NET (Nov. 6, 2008), http://www.scidev.net/en/news/kenya-prepares-to-approve-biosafety-legislation.html.

[19] JUDI W. WAKHUNGU & DAVID K. WAFULA, INTRODUCING BT COTTON: POLICY LESSONS FOR SMALLHOLDER FARMERS IN KENYA 43 (2004).

[20] KAREMBU ET AL., *supra* note 5, at 15.

Kenya issued the National Biotechnology Development Policy.[21] The Bill was finally enacted in 2009 and put into effect in 2011.[22]

II. The Biosafety Act

The Biosafety Act of 2009 establishes a comprehensive legal framework for governing activities related to GMOs and seeks to correct the problems that made the provisional regulatory framework ineffective. As indicated in the Memorandum of Objects and Reasons that Sally Kosgel, the Minister of Higher Education, Science, and Technology, submitted to Parliament along with the 2008 version of the Bill, the Biosafety Act domesticates the Cartagena Protocol and implements the 2006 National Biotechnology Development Policy.[23]

This new legal framework does two things: it encourages the exploitation of biotechnology in Kenya by putting in place mechanisms for expanding biotechnology-related activities in the country, including environmental release and commercialization of GMOs already developed, and it seeks to ensure that the development and exploitation of biotechnology in Kenya is effectively regulated in order to minimize the risk of adverse effects associated with the industry. This is evident in the tone and language of the Act, which lists the following objectives:

a) to facilitate responsible research into, and minimize the risks that may be posed by, genetically modified organisms;
b) to ensure an adequate level of protection for the safe transfer, handling and use of genetically modified organisms that may have an adverse effect on the health of the people and the environment; and
c) to establish a transparent, science-based and predictable process for reviewing and making decisions on the transfer, handling and use of genetically modified organisms and related activities.[24]

To this end the Act establishes a regulatory agency, the National Biosafety Authority (NBA).[25] Part of the Ministry of Higher Education, Science, and Technology, the NBA is managed by a board consisting of representatives of relevant government institutions; scientists; and persons representing the interests of farmers, consumers, and the biotechnology industry.[26] The NBA's mandate is to supervise and control the transfer, handling, and use of GMOs with the purpose of safeguarding human and animal health as well as the environment.[27]

---

[21] REPUBLIC OF KENYA, *supra* note 1.

[22] The Biosafety Act, No. 2 (2009), § 1, version including commencement date *available at* http://www.kenyalaw.org/kenyalaw/klr_home/index.php.

[23] The Biosafety Bill, 2008, Memorandum of Objects and Reasons, at 44 (June 24, 2008), *available at* http://www.kenya law.org/klr/fileadmin/pdfdownloads/Bills/2008/The_Biosafety_Bill_2008.pdf.

[24] The Biosafety Act § 4.

[25] *Id.* § 5.

[26] *Id.* § 6; *Welcome to National Biosafety Authority*, NBA, http://www.biosafetykenya.go ke/ (last visited Aug. 30, 2012).

[27] The Biosafety Act § 7.

In carrying out its functions, the NBA has many eyes and ears. The Act permits NBA biosafety inspectors to monitor compliance with the Act and its regulations.[28] In addition, as part of the NBA's duty to coordinate all activities relating to GMOs, its staff works with eight designated regulatory agencies, the majority of which are represented on the NBA board, to provide assistance in monitoring GMO-related activities: the Department of Public Health, the Department of Veterinary Services, the Kenya Bureau of Standards, the Kenya Plant Health Inspectorate Services, the Kenya Industrial Property Institute, the Kenya Wildlife Service, the Pest Control Products Board, and the National Environment Management Authority.[29] These agencies work with the NBA to, among other duties, monitor approved GMO-related activities for compliance with the laws and conditions imposed by the NBA.[30]

The NBA's powers also include issuing cessation and restoration orders. The NBA can order an immediate cessation if a "person issued with an approval" for a biotechnological activity fails to demonstrate compliance with its terms "after a reasonable period of time" or fails to comply with the provisions of the Act as well as its regulations.[31] In addition, the NBA has the authority to issue an environmental restoration order whenever there is a release of GMOs into the environment.[32] The responsible party may be required either to restore the environment to the condition it was in prior to the GMOs' release or to pay for the needed restoration.[33]

The Act imposes criminal sanctions for violating its provisions or the terms attached to an approval order by the NBA. Anyone who uses, releases into the environment, commercializes, or imports or exports GMOs without first obtaining an approval order from the NBA commits an offense and is, on conviction, punishable by a fine of up to KSH20 million (about US$238,000) and/or a maximum of ten years' imprisonment.[34] Failure to provide information required by the Act, use of GMOs in a manner not consistent with an approval order issued by the NBA, use of GMOs for unethical purposes, or obstructing or failing to cooperate with the NBA are also offenses and carry similar penalties.[35]

III. Regulations

The Act envisages at least six regulations for implementing its provisions. Four regulations have already been issued.[36] These regulations establish specific procedures for various activities involving GMOs: environmental release; import, export, and transit; contained use; and labeling.

---

[28] *Id.* §§ 43–44.

[29] *Id.*, First Schedule.

[30] *Id.* § 38.

[31] *Id.* § 42.

[32] *Id.* § 40.

[33] *Id.*

[34] *Id.* § 52.

[35] *Id.*

[36] *Biosafety Regulations*, NBA, http://www.biosafetykenya.go ke/index.php?option=com_content&view=category&layout=blog&id=84&Itemid=498 (last visited Aug. 30, 2012).

A. Regulations on Environmental Release

The Biosafety (Environmental Release) Regulations put in place procedures for obtaining an approval order from the NBA for the release of GMOs into the environment and their introduction into the market. The Regulations also provide the necessary forms for filing an application for approval.[37] An approval order is good for ten years and may be renewed.[38]

The Regulations also impose a strict ban on the NBA's release to a third party of confidential information that it receives in the course of the application approval process.[39]

B. Regulations on Import, Export, and Transit

The Biosafety (Import, Export and Transit) Regulations were issued to ensure that GMOs are moved into, across, and out of Kenya without posing risks to human health and the environment. The Regulations provide that any import, export, or transit of GMOs requires prior NBA approval.[40]

Notable provisions in the Regulations set up a protocol to be followed in the event of unauthorized importation or transit of a GMO. In such a situation, the NBA is required to "initiate remedial actions," including refusing to grant entry/transit, destruction of the GMO, or setting the conditions for use/transit.[41] The NBA may also "inform and advise" the public regarding the particular GMOs.[42]

In addition, the Regulations put in place procedures for dealing with the accidental release of GMOs in transit into the environment.[43]

C. Regulations on Contained Use

The Biosafety (Contained Use) Regulations establish four containment levels for GMO-related activities, ranging from activities with no or negligible risk to high-risk activities.[44] The NBA, in consultation with the relevant regulatory agency, determines the containment level of premises intended for the contained use of GMOs.[45]

---

[37] The Biosafety (Environmental Release) Regulations, 2011, *supra* note 3, §§ 5–6.

[38] *Id.* § 10.

[39] *Id.* § 16.

[40] The Biosafety (Import, Export and Transit) Regulations, 2011, *supra* note 3, §§ 4, 6–7.

[41] *Id.* § 5.

[42] *Id.*

[43] *Id.* § 10.

[44] The Biosafety (Contained Use) Regulations, 2011, *supra* note 3, § 5.

[45] *Id.*

The Regulations impose two notable conditions. Before obtaining an approval order, applicants for a contained use are required to put in place a contingency plan for mitigating risk in the event of failure of the contained-use measures.[46] The Regulations also mandate that any research institution engaging in the contained use of GMOs must establish an Institutional Biosafety Committee.[47] The functions of this Committee include preparing applications for contained-use activities and assisting the institution in establishing monitoring mechanisms for risk assessment and management.[48]

D. Regulations on Labeling

The Biosafety (Labeling) Regulations have two objectives. First, they seek to ensure that information regarding genetically modified food, feed, or any other product is disseminated to the public so that consumers are able to make informed decisions.[49] Second, they improve the traceability of genetically modified products and this, among other aims, facilitates implementation of risk-management measures.[50]

There are, however, a few exemptions from the labeling requirements. The Regulations do not apply to food, feed, or their ingredients and derived products if the GMOs present in them constitute less than 1% of their total weight; highly refined food from which novel DNA or novel proteins are removed during processing; processing aids or food additives, unless novel DNA or novel proteins present in the food with such additives are above the threshold level of 1%; or "food intended for consumption prepared and sold from food premises and vendors."[51]

Prepared by Hanibal Goitom
Foreign Law Specialist
September 2012

---

[46] *Id.* § 13.

[47] *Id.* § 6.

[48] *Id.*

[49] The Biosafety (Labeling) Regulations, 2012, *supra* note 3, § 3; *Labeling Regulations*, NBA, http://www.biosafetykenya.go.ke/index.php?option=com_content&view=article&id=163:biosafety-labeling-regulations-2012&catid=84&Itemid=498.

[50] The Biosafety (Labeling) Regulations, 2012, *supra* note 3, § 3.

[51] *Id.* § 5.

LAW LIBRARY OF CONGRESS

NEW ZEALAND

REGULATION OF GENETICALLY MODIFIED ORGANISMS

Executive Summary

    The development and release of genetically modified organisms is strictly controlled in New Zealand. There is ongoing discussion regarding the economic benefits, environmental concerns, risks to human health, and cultural and spiritual considerations associated with biotechnology. The relevant legislation requires these issues to be considered in decision making related to genetically modified organisms, and approvals may be granted only where the benefits outweigh the risks. The law clearly states that a precautionary approach is to be taken in managing the potential adverse effects of such organisms.

I. Introduction

    There is a high level of controversy in New Zealand relating to the development and use of genetically modified organisms in the context of crops and farm animals.[1] The debate includes public opinion and political stances regarding the economic benefits[2] of genetic engineering as opposed to those gained from protecting New Zealand's "clean, green image,"[3] as well as questions about the environmental risks from genetic modification,[4] the impact on human health, and consideration of spiritual and cultural values, particularly the perspectives of Māori.[5]

---

[1] *See GM Fight Still Rages 20 Years On*, TVNZ (Nov. 29, 2008), http://tvnz.co.nz/health-news/gm-fight-still-rages-20-years-2340450.

[2] *See* THE TREASURY, ECONOMIC RISKS AND OPPORTUNITIES FROM THE RELEASE OF GENETICALLY MODIFIED ORGANISMS IN NEW ZEALAND (Apr. 17, 2003), http://www.treasury.govt nz/economy/reports/gmo.

[3] *See* Joanna Gamble, *Genetic Engineering: The New Zealand Public's Point of View*, The University of Auckland (2001), https://researchspace.auckland.ac.nz/handle/2292/863; Doug Ashwell & Su Olsson, *"To Be or Not To Be": An Analysis of Political Rhetoric in the New Zealand Debate on Genetic Modification*, AUSTRALIA AND NEW ZEALAND COMMUNICATION ASSOCIATION ONLINE JOURNAL (2002), http://www hss.bond.edu.au/ANZCA/papers/SOlssonDAshwellPaper-.pdf; Pauline Hamilton, *GE or Not GE: The Genetic Engineering Debate in New Zealand*, 31(12) CHEMICAL INNOVATION (Dec. 2001), http://pubs.acs.org/subscribe/archive/ci/31/i12/html/12vp html.

[4] *See About Genetic Modification*, MINISTRY FOR THE ENVIRONMENT, http://www mfe.govt nz/issues/organisms/about-gm/index html (last visited Aug. 23, 2012).

[5] *See generally* Parliamentary Library, Background Note: Genetic Modification (Feb. 21, 2002), http://www.parliament nz/NR/rdonlyres/42B8A108-0670-4C7E-B242-5D430E6BC1AF/370/0201Geneticmodification1.pdf; Dana Rachelle Peterson, Genetic Modification: A Resource Document for MPs (Parliamentary Library Background Paper No. 26, Feb. 2002), http://www.parliament nz/NR/rdonlyres/4CA0C507-3047-486B-8E6C-DFEBE9AB761E/416/BP26 GeneticModification3.pdf.

As a result of this discussion, and the regulatory approaches that have been developed in an attempt to address and balance the various concerns and interests, there is a great deal of information and analysis available on the subject of genetic modification, ethics, and the law in New Zealand.[6]

II. Regulatory Framework for Approval of Genetically Modified Organisms

New Zealand "maintains one of the most comprehensive and rigorous approval regimes for genetically modified organisms in the world."[7] The importation, development, testing, and release of "new organisms," including genetically modified organisms, are regulated by the Hazardous Substances and New Organisms Act 1996 (HSNO Act).[8] When the legislation was first enacted in 1996 it represented "one of the most significant reforms of environmental legislation since the Resource Management Act."[9]

The HSNO Act is administered by the Ministry for the Environment,[10] while the Environmental Protection Authority (EPA) is responsible for implementing the provisions relating to the application and assessment process for new organisms.[11] Other agencies are also responsible for enforcement and compliance and for the implementation of other relevant legislation.[12]

---

[6] For general background information, *see* Daryl Macer et al., *Genetic Engineering in New Zealand: Science, Ethics and Public Policy* (Centre for Resource Management, Lincoln University, Information Paper No. 27, 1991), http://dspace.lincoln.ac.nz/dspace/bitstream/10182/1108/1/crm_ip_27.pdf; *see also* MINISTRY FOR THE ENVIRONMENT, GENETIC MODIFICATION: THE NEW ZEALAND APPROACH (June 2004), http://www.mfe.govt.nz/publications/organisms/gm-nz-approach-jun04/genetic-modification-nz-approach.pdf; Paul Havemann, *Genetic Modification, Ecological Good Governance and the Law: New Zealand in the Age of Risk*, 10 JAMES COOK U. L. REV. 7 (2003), http://www.austlii.edu.au/au/journals/JCULRev/2003/2.html. A list of government publications on new and genetically modified organisms is available on the Ministry for the Environment website *at* http://www.mfe.govt.nz/publications/organisms/ (last visited Aug. 20, 2012).

[7] USDA FOREIGN AGRICULTURAL SERVICE, GAIN REPORT: NEW ZEALAND – BIOTECHNOLOGY – GE PLANTS AND ANIMALS (July 15, 2010), http://gain.fas.usda.gov/Recent%20GAIN%20Publications/Biotechnology%20-%20GE%20Plants%20and%20Animals_Wellington_New%20Zealand_7-15-2010.pdf.

[8] Hazardous Substances and New Organisms Act 1996, http://www.legislation.govt.nz/act/public/1996/0030/latest/DLM381222.html.

[9] *Hazardous Substances and New Organisms (HSNO) Act 1996*, MINISTRY FOR THE ENVIRONMENT, http://www.mfe.govt.nz/laws/hsno.html (last visited Aug. 23, 2012).

[10] Ministry for the Environment, HSNO Information Sheet 5: Who is Responsible for the New Act?, http://www.mfe.govt.nz/publications/hazardous/info-sheets-dec97/info-sheet-5-dec97.html (last visited Aug. 20, 2012). This refers to the role of ERMA (the Environmental Risk Management Authority), which was replaced by the Environmental Protection Agency (EPA) in 2011.

[11] *See What We Do: Hazardous Substances and New Organisms*, EPA, http://www.epa.govt.nz/about-us/what/Pages/Hazardous-substances-and-new-organisms.aspx (last visited Aug. 20, 2012).

[12] *See generally, How Genetic Modification is Regulated in New Zealand*, MINISTRY FOR THE ENVIRONMENT, http://www.mfe.govt.nz/issues/organisms/regulation/gm-regulation.html; *Importing Genetically Modified Organisms*, MINISTRY FOR PRIMARY INDUSTRIES, http://www.biosecurity.govt.nz/regs/imports/plants/gmo; *Our Role in Enforcement*, EPA, http://www.epa.govt.nz/about-us/what/Pages/EPA-role-enforcement.aspx (all last visited Aug. 24, 2012).

The preliminary provisions in the HSNO Act set out key principles and relevant matters that must be taken into account in the exercise of decision-making functions under the Act. The wording of these provisions reflect the various societal interests and concerns associated with new and genetically modified organisms, and require a detailed assessment of risks and benefits:

4 Purpose of Act
The purpose of this Act is to protect the environment, and the health and safety of people and communities, by preventing or managing the adverse effects of hazardous substances and new organisms.

5 Principles relevant to purpose of Act
All persons exercising functions, powers, and duties under this Act shall, to achieve the purpose of this Act, recognise and provide for the following principles:
>   (a) the safeguarding of the life-supporting capacity of air, water, soil, and ecosystems:
>   (b) the maintenance and enhancement of the capacity of people and communities to provide for their own economic, social, and cultural well-being and for the reasonably foreseeable needs of future generations.

6 Matters relevant to purpose of Act
All persons exercising functions, powers, and duties under this Act shall, to achieve the purpose of this Act, take into account the following matters:
>   (a) the sustainability of all native and valued introduced flora and fauna:
>   (b) the intrinsic value of ecosystems:
>   (c) public health:
>   (d) the relationship of Maori and their culture and traditions with their ancestral lands, water, sites, waahi tapu, valued flora and fauna, and other taonga:
>   (e) the economic and related benefits and costs of using a particular hazardous substance or new organism:
>   (f) New Zealand's international obligations.

7 Precautionary approach
All persons exercising functions, powers, and duties under this Act, including but not limited to, functions, powers, and duties under sections 28A, 29, 32, 38, 45, and 48, shall take into account the need for caution in managing adverse effects where there is scientific and technical uncertainty about those effects.[13]

Section 7 refers to some of the various determinations that the EPA can make under the HSNO Act.[14] The provisions relating to these determinations also include particular requirements regarding the protection of the environment and human health and safety. For example, every application for the development or field testing in containment of a genetically modified organism must provide information on "all the possible adverse effects of the organism on the environment."[15] In addition, the EPA must take into account any adverse effects on "human health and safety" and "the environment, in particular ecosystems and their constituent

---

[13] Hazardous Substances and New Organisms Act 1996, ss 4-7.

[14] *Id.* s 27.

[15] *Id.* ss 34(2)(e), 40(2)(a)(v), 40(2)(b)(v).

parts," as well as alternative methods for achieving the research objective and "any effects resulting from the transfer of any genetic elements to other organisms in or around the site of the development or field test."[16]

Other legislation that relates to the control of genetically modified organisms includes the Biosecurity Act 1993,[17] which provides for the "exclusion, eradication and management of pests and other unwanted organisms in New Zealand – including GM organisms."[18] In addition, any food that is genetically modified or contains genetically modified material must be approved by Food Standards Australia New Zealand[19] and must be clearly labeled.[20] The use of animals in research and testing is strictly regulated by the Animal Welfare Act 1999,[21] with every project required to be approved and monitored by an animal ethics committee and to only be conducted by organizations that follow an approved ethical code of conduct.[22]

III. Consideration of Māori Perspectives

In addition to the preliminary provisions to the HSNO Act described above, which require that consideration be given to "the relationship of Maori and their culture and traditions with their ancestral lands, water, sites, waahi tapu [sacred place], valued flora and fauna, and other taonga [treasures, both tangible and intangible]," the legislation also states that "[a]ll persons exercising powers and functions under this Act shall take into account the principles of the Treaty of Waitangi (Te Tiriti o Waitangi)."[23] Similar "Treaty clauses" are included in various pieces of legislation in New Zealand and have both legal and symbolic meaning. The clause prevents the Crown and its representatives from acting inconsistently with obligations to Māori and related principles that have been interpreted as applying under the Treaty of Waitangi signed between Māori tribes and the British Crown in 1840.[24]

---

[16] *Id.* s 44A.

[17] Biosecurity Act 1993, http://www.legislation.govt nz/act/public/1993/0095/latest/DLM314623.html.

[18] *How Genetic Modification is Regulated in New Zealand, supra* note 12.

[19] *See* FOOD STANDARDS AUSTRALIA NEW ZEALAND, http://www.foodstandards.gov.au/.

[20] *See* Ministry of Agriculture and Forestry, Genetically Modified Food and Ingredients (updated Jan. 1, 2012), http://www foodsafety.govt nz/elibrary/industry/Genetically_Modified-Expectations_Importers.pdf; *Genetically Modified Food,* MINISTRY FOR PRIMARY INDUSTRIES, http://www foodsmart.govt.nz/whats-in-our-food/genetically-modifed-food/ (last visited Aug. 24, 2012). Standard 1.5.2 of the Australia New Zealand Food Standards Code, http://www.comlaw.gov.au/Details/F2012C00518, outlines the legal requirements for the sale and labeling of food produced using gene technology.

[21] Animal Welfare Act 1999, pt 6, http://www.legislation.govt.nz/act/public/1999/0142/latest/DLM49664 html; *see generally*

[22] *Animals in Research,* Ministry for Primary Industries, http://www.biosecurity.govt nz/regs/animal-welfare/research (last visited Aug. 21, 2012).

[23] Hazardous Substances and New Organisms Act 1996, s 8.

[24] *See* Janine Hayward, *Appendix: The Principles of the Treaty of Waitangi, in* 2 WAITANGI TRIBUNAL, RANGAHAUA WHANUI: NATIONAL OVERVIEW 475-94 (Alan Ward, ed. 1997), *available at* http://www.waitangi-tribunal.govt.nz/doclibrary/public/Appendix%2899%29.pdf. In particular, four principles can be said to have emerged from Treaty jurisprudence: "the principle of active protection, the tribal right to self-regulation, the right of

The notions of partnership and a duty to consult are reflected in legal and practical approaches to seeking the views of Māori on applications relating to new organisms. In particular, a Māori Advisory Committee is established under the Environmental Protection Authority Act 2011 (EPA Act).[25] The role of the Committee is to "provide advice and assistance to the EPA on matters relating to policy, process, and decisions of the EPA under an environmental Act or this Act" from a Māori perspective.[26] The EPA also engages directly with the Māori community and requires applicants to do so as well.[27] The EPA is currently developing a policy document on engaging with Māori.[28]

IV. Royal Commission on Genetic Modification

Various aspects of the HSNO Act relating to genetically modified organisms were incorporated through amending legislation that was passed in 2003, including provisions relating to the conditional release of new organisms, a civil liability and pecuniary penalties regime,[29] as well as the original requirement to establish a Māori advisory committee.[30] The amendments

---

redress for past breaches, and the duty to consult." *Principles of the Treaty*, WAITANGI TRIBUNAL, http://www.waitangi-tribunal.govt.nz/treaty/principles.asp (last visited Aug. 21, 2012).

[25] Environmental Protection Authority Act 2011, s 18, http://www.legislation.govt.nz/act/public/2011/0014/latest/DLM3366813 html. Previously, a 2003 amendment to the HSNO Act introduced a statutory requirement for a Māori advisory committee to ERMA, but the relevant provisions were repealed in 2011 and replaced with provisions in the Environmental Protection Authority Act 2011. *See* ERMA New Zealand Information Sheet: The HSNO Act and Māori (Sept. 2006), http://www.epa.govt.nz/Publications/ER-IS-17-04-0906.pdf; *Spiritual, Cultural and Ethical Issues in Genetic Modification*, MINISTRY FOR THE ENVIRONMENT, http://www mfe.govt nz/publications/organisms/gm-nz-approach-jun04/html/page5 html (last visited Aug. 25, 2012).

[26] Environmental Protection Authority Act 2011, s 19. For information on Māori perspectives relating to genetically modified organisms, *see* Jessica Hutchings, *Te Whakaruruhau, Te Ukaipo: Mana Wahine and Genetic Modification* Ch 5: GM and Māori (Unpublished PhD Thesis, Victoria University of Wellington, 2002), http://www kaupapamaori.com/assets//HutchingsJ/te whakaruruhau chpt5.pdf; Mere Roberts & John R. Fairweather, *South Island Maori Perceptions of Biotechnology* (Research Report No. 268, Lincoln University, Sept. 2004), http://dspace.lincoln.ac.nz/dspace/bitstream/10182/745/1/aeru rr 268.pdf.

[27] *See Te Hautū: What We do*, EPA, http://www.epa.govt nz/about-us/te-hautu/what-we-do/Pages/What%20we%20do.aspx.

[28] *Engaging with Māori Draft Policy*, EPA, http://www.epa.govt.nz/consultations/general/Pages/Engaging-with Maori-draft-policy.aspx. Other government agencies with a role in the regulation of genetically modified organisms also engage with Māori as part of decision-making processes. *See, e.g., Māori and Biosecurity*, MINISTRY FOR PRIMARY INDUSTRIES, http://www.biosecurity.govt nz/about-us/maori (last visited Aug. 24, 2012).

[29] In addition to compliance orders and fines for various infringement offences in part 7, the HSNO Act includes pecuniary penalties and civil liability provisions in Part 7A. *See Liability for Genetic Modification*, MINISTRY FOR THE ENVIRONMENT, http://www.mfe.govt.nz/issues/organisms/regulation/liability.html (last visited Aug. 24, 2012).

[30] *Law Changes for New and Genetically Modified Organisms: Background to the Law Changes for Genetically Modified Organisms*, MINISTRY FOR THE ENVIRONMENT, http://www.mfe.govt.nz/issues/organisms/law-changes/ (last visited Aug. 20, 2012).

resulted from the government's response[31] to the report of a Royal Commission on Genetic Modification, which was established in 2000 and completed its report in July 2001.[32]

The major conclusion of the Royal Commission was that New Zealand should proceed cautiously with genetic modification, but not completely "close the door" to it.[33] More than 10,000 written submissions from members of the public were received as part of the Royal Commission process.[34] During this time, a two-year moratorium on applications to release genetically modified organisms was in effect.[35] The moratorium expired on October 29, 2003, when the HSNO Act amendments came into force.[36] Protesters held marches and rallies against the lifting of the moratorium, while the biotechnology industry and farmers welcomed the move.[37]

The Royal Commission recommended the establishment of a Bioethics Council to "provide advice and promote ongoing dialogue among New Zealanders" regarding the cultural, ethical and spiritual aspects of biotechnology.[38] This body began work in 2002 and was disestablished in March 2009.[39]

V. Current Situation

Currently, there are no genetically modified commercial crops being grown in New Zealand, and no fresh produce or meat sold that is genetically modified.[40] Genetic modification

---

[31] *Royal Commission on Genetic Modification: The Government Response*, MINISTRY FOR THE ENVIRONMENT, http://www.mfe.govt.nz/issues/organisms/law-changes/commission/ (last visited Aug. 20, 2012).

[32] REPORT OF THE ROYAL COMMISSION ON GENETIC MODIFICATION (2002), *available at* http://www.mfe.govt.nz/publications/organisms/royal-commission-gm/index.html.

[33] *Genetic Modification Regulation*, MINISTRY FOR THE ENVIRONMENT, http://www.mfe.govt.nz/issues/organisms/regulation/index.html (last visited Aug. 27, 2012). *See also* Allan Coukell, *A Step Forward for Genetic Engineering in New Zealand*, N.Y. TIMES (Aug. 21, 2001), http://www.nytimes.com/2001/08/21/science/a-step-forward-for-genetic-engineering-in-new-zealand.html.

[34] *Genetic Modification Regulation*, *supra* note 33.

[35] *See* Press Release, Hon. Pete Hodgson, GM Research Moratorium Keeps NZ's Options Open (Apr. 17, 2000), http://www.beehive.govt.nz/release/gm-research-moratorium-keeps-nz039s-options-open.

[36] Press Release, Hon. Marian Hobbs, New GM Legislation in Force as Moratorium Expires (Oct. 29, 2003), http://www.beehive.govt.nz/node/18221.

[37] *See* Kevin Taylor, *Government Opens Door to GE Despite Protests, Polls and Threats*, NEW ZEALAND HERALD (Oct. 29, 2003), http://www.nzherald.co.nz/nz/news/article.cfm?c_id=1&objectid=3531306.

[38] *Other Work: Toi te Taiao: The Bioethics Council*, MINISTRY FOR THE ENVIRONMENT, http://www.mfe.govt.nz/issues/organisms/other-work/index.html (last visited Aug. 27, 2012).

[39] *Id.* Publications of the Bioethics Council are now available on the National Library website at http://ndhadeliver.natlib.govt.nz/ArcAggregator/arcView/IE1074184/http://www.bioethics.org.nz/publications/index.html with harvested websites *available at* http://ndhadeliver.natlib.govt.nz/content-aggregator/getIEs?system=ilsdb&id=1287327 (last visited Aug. 27, 2012).

[40] *See Labelling & Safety – Questions & Answers*, MINISTRY FOR PRIMARY INDUSTRIES, http://www.foodsmart.govt.nz/whats-in-our-food/genetically-modifed-food/labelling/questions-answers.htm (last visited Aug. 20, 2012).

techniques are used in research in contained environments, for example in relation to pest control, pharmaceutical research, and the enhancement of the production capacity of crops and animals.[41] There have been reports of various controversies in recent years relating to the development and potential release of genetically modified organisms. For example, there was debate and legal proceedings related to research involving farm animals,[42] including the approval for a trial involving putting synthetic human genes into goats, sheep, and cows to see if they would produce human proteins in their milk;[43] and genetically modified pine trees that had been contained at a research center were recently destroyed by protesters.[44] Although there is also some discussion about the potential impact of the strict controls on genetically modified organisms on economic development,[45] "there have been no official changes to the heavily regulated and cautious policy settings operated by the New Zealand Government in relation to biotechnology."[46]

Prepared by Kelly Buchanan
Chief, Foreign, Comparative, and
International Law Division I
September 2012

---

[41] *How Genetic Modification is Being Used in New Zealand Research*, MINISTRY FOR THE ENVIRONMENT, http://www.mfe.govt nz/issues/organisms/about-gm/research html (last visited Aug. 27, 2012). *See also Field Tests and Outdoor Developments of Genetically Modified Organisms,* EPA, http://epa.govt.nz/new-organisms/popular-no-topics/Pages/GM-field-tests-in-NZ.aspx (last visited Aug. 27, 2012); USDA FOREIGN AGRICULTURAL SERVICE, GAIN REPORT: NEW ZEALAND – AGRICULTURAL BIOTECHNOLOGY ANNUAL REPORT (July 15, 2011), http://gain.fas.usda.gov/Recent%20GAIN%20Publications/Agricultural%20Biotechnology%20Annual_Wellington_New%20Zealand_7-15-2011.pdf.

[42] Branwen Morgan, *New Zealand's GM Cattle Under Fire*, NATURE (Mar. 27, 2010), http://www.nature.com/news/2010/100327/full/news.2010.155 html.

[43] Eloise Gibson, *Human Genes to be Injected into Goats, Cows, and Sheep*, NEW ZEALAND HERALD (Apr. 16, 2010), http://www.nzherald.co nz/nz/news/article.cfm?c_id=1&objectid=10638717; Eloise Gibson, *Mutant Cows Die in GM Trial*, NEW ZEALAND HERALD (May 1, 2010), http://www.nzherald.co.nz/nz/news/article.cfm?c_id=1&objectid=10642031.

[44] Tony Reid, *GM Modified Pine Trees Destroyed in Raid*, 3NEWS (Apr. 13, 2012), http://www.3news.co nz/GM-modified-pine-trees-destroyed-in-raid/tabid/1160/articleID/250349/Default.aspx; *Hundreds of GM Trees Destroyed*, STUFF.CO.NZ (Apr. 13, 2004), http://www.stuff.co.nz/national/6735584/Hundreds-of-GM-trees-destroyed; Paul Harper, *GE Tree Attack: Company Vows to Replant*, NEW ZEALAND HERALD (Apr. 13, 2012), http://www.nzherald.co.nz/nz/news/article.cfm?c_id=1&objectid=10798491.

[45] *See, e.g.,* Paul Gorman, *GM Trials' Failure 'Not Law's Fault'*, STUFF.CO.NZ (Apr. 12, 2012), http://www.stuff.co.nz/business/farming/6732484/GM-trials-failure-not-laws-fault; David Fisher, *GE Law Probe a Big Surprise*, NEW ZEALAND HERALD (Nov. 20, 2011), http://www.nzherald.co.nz/nz/news/article.cfm?c_id=1&objectid=10767413.

[46] USDA FOREIGN AGRICULTURAL SERVICE, GAIN REPORT: NEW ZEALAND – BIOTECHNOLOGY STILL AT A CROSSROADS IN NEW ZEALAND (July 15, 2012), http://gain.fas.usda.gov/Recent%20GAIN%20Publications/Agricultural%20Biotechnology%20Annual_Wellington_New%20Zealand_7-24-2012.pdf.

LAW LIBRARY OF CONGRESS

BRAZIL

BIOETHICS

Executive Summary

According to the Brazilian Constitution, everyone has the right to an ecologically balanced environment. The government and the people are charged with the duty of defending and preserving the environment, and it is the responsibility of the government to preserve the diversity and integrity of the country's genetic patrimony and to supervise the entities dedicated to research and manipulation of genetic material.

Under this principle, Brazil has enacted laws to regulate the use of genetic engineering and has created commissions designed to help prepare and implement a National Biosafety Policy, which has yet to be published.

I. Legal Framework

The Brazilian Constitution imposes on the government and the people the duty to defend and preserve the environment.[1] To this effect, on January 5, 1995, Brazil promulgated Law No. 8,974, which regulated this Constitutional principle, established rules for the use of genetic engineering techniques and the release of genetically modified organisms into the environment, and created the National Technical Commission on Biosafety (*Comissão Técnica Nacional de Biossegurança – CTNBio*).[2]   On December 20, 1995, Decree No. 1,752 was enacted to regulate Law No. 8,974 and to provide for the duties and composition of the CTNBio.[3]

On March 24, 2005, Law No. 11,105 was promulgated to implement article 225(§1)(II), (IV), and (V) of the Constitution. Law No. 11,105 establishes safety standards and enforcement mechanisms for activities involving genetically modified organisms and their derivatives, creates the National Biosafety Council (*Conselho Nacional de Biossegurança – CNBS*), restructures the CTNBio, provides for the National Biosafety Policy (*Política Nacional de Biossegurança –*

---

[1] CONSTITUIÇÃO FEDERAL [C.F.] art. 225, http://www.planalto.gov.br/ccivil_03/Constituicao/Constituiçao.htm. For the purposes of Law No. 6,938 of August 31, 1981, which provides for the National Environmental Policy, article 3(I) defines "environment" as "the set of conditions, laws, influences, and interactions of physical, chemical, and biological order, which permit, shelter, and govern life in all its forms." Lei No. 6.938, de 31 de Agosto de 1981, http://www.planalto.gov.br/ccivil_03/Leis/L6938_htm (translation by author).

[2] Lei No. 8.974, de 5 de Janeiro de 1995, https://www.planalto.gov.br/ccivil_03/leis/l8974_htm.

[3] Decreto No. 1.752, de 20 de Dezembro de 1995, https://www.planalto.gov.br/ccivil_03/decreto/D1752_htm.

PNB), and revokes Law 8,974 of January 5, 1995.[4] To regulate Law No. 11,105, on November 22, 2005, the government issued Decree No. 5,591, which also establishes rules for the use of human stem cells for the purposes of research and therapy.[5]

II. Current Law

A. Constitutional Principle

The Brazilian Constitution determines that everyone has the right to an ecologically balanced environment, which is a public good for the people's use and is essential for a healthy life. The Government and the community have a duty to defend and to preserve the environment for present and future generations.[6] To assure the effectiveness of this right, it is the responsibility of the Government to preserve the diversity and integrity of the country's genetic patrimony and to supervise entities dedicated to research and manipulation of genetic material;[7] to require, as provided by law, a prior environmental impact study, which must be made public, for installation of works or activities that may cause significant degradation of the environment;[8] and to control the production, commercialization, and employment of techniques, methods and substances that carry a risk to life, the quality of life, and the environment.[9]

B. Law No. 11,105 of March 24, 2005

Law No. 11,105 regulates article 225(§1)(II), (IV), and (V) of the Constitution by establishing safety norms and inspection mechanisms for the construction, culture, production, manipulation, transportation, transfer, import, export, storage, research, commercialization, consumption, environmental release and discharge of genetically modified organisms and their by-products.[10] The stimulus to scientific advances in the area of biosafety and biotechnology, protection of life, human health, and the health of animals and plants, as well as the observance of the precautionary principle for the protection of the environment, were used as guidelines to draft the law.[11]

Activities and projects involving genetically modified organisms and their by-products are limited to public and private entities which are responsible for the compliance with Law No. 11,105 and its regulation as well as the eventual consequences or effects resulting from

---

[4] Lei No. 11.105, de 24 de Março de 2005, http://www.planalto.gov.br/ccivil_03/_Ato2004-2006/2005/Lei/L11105 htm#art42.

[5] Decreto No. 5.591, de 22 de Novembro de 2005, http://www.planalto.gov.br/ccivil_03/_Ato2004-2006/2005/Decreto/D5591.htm.

[6] C.F. art. 225.

[7] *Id.* art. 225(§1)(II).

[8] *Id.* art. 225(§1)(IV).

[9] *Id.* art. 225(§1)(V).

[10] Lei No. 11.105, *supra* note 4, art. 1.

[11] *Id.*

noncompliance.[12] Individuals acting in an autonomous and independent capacity are not allowed to develop activities and projects involving genetically modified organisms.[13]

Stem Cell Research and Therapy

The use of embryonic stem cells obtained from human embryos produced by in vitro fertilization and not used in the procedure is permitted for research and therapy, provided that the embryos are not viable;[14] the embryos had been frozen for three years or more on the date of publication of Law No. 11,105; or the embryos were already frozen on the date of publication of Law No. 11,105, and subsequently attained the three-year mark.[15] In any case, consent of the parents is required.[16]

Research institutions and health services that undertake research or therapy with human embryonic stem cells must submit their projects to the respective research ethics committees for consideration and approval,[17] in keeping with the resolution of the National Council of Health (*Conselho Nacional de Saúde – CNS*).[18] The commercialization of biological material referred to in article 5 of Law No. 11,105 is forbidden and its practice is qualified as a crime, as defined in article 15 of Law 9,434 of February 4, 1997.[19]

Law No. 11,105 prohibits, inter alia, genetic engineering of living organisms or in vitro handling of natural or recombinant DNA/RNA performed in breach of the rules established in Law No. 11,105;[20] genetic engineering of human germinal cells, human zygotes, and human embryos;[21] and human cloning.[22] It is mandatory that all accidents that occur during the course of research and projects in the area of genetic engineering be investigated and that a report be sent to the competent authority within five days from the date of the event.[23]

---

[12] *Id.* art. 2.

[13] *Id.* art. 2(§2).

[14] *Id.* art. 5(I).

[15] *Id.* art. 5(II).

[16] *Id.* art. 5(§1).

[17] *Id.* art. 5(§2).

[18] Decreto No. 5.591, *supra* note 5, art. 63(§2). Decree No. 5,591 further regulates the research and therapy that uses human embryonic stem cells by establishing civil and administrative responsibilities (art. 68), administrative infringements (art. 69), administrative sanctions (arts. 70–79), and administrative procedure (arts. 80–84).

[19] Lei No. 11.105, *supra* note 4, art. 5(§3). Article 15 of Law No. 9,434 of February 4, 1997, considers as a crime the act of purchasing or selling human tissue, organs, or parts of the human body, which are punishable by three to eight years in prison and a fine. The same punishment applies to whoever promotes, mediates, facilitates, or receives any advantage from the transaction. Lei No. 9.434 de 4 de Fevereiro de 1997, http://www.planalto.gov.br/ccivil_03/LEIS/L9434.htm#art15.

[20] Lei No. 11.105, *supra* note 4, art. 6(II).

[21] *Id.* art. 6(III).

[22] *Id.* art. 6(IV).

[23] *Id.* art. 7(I).

On October 10, 1996, CNS issued Resolution No. 196,[24] which approved the guidelines and regulating norms regarding research that involves human beings.[25] Article II of the Resolution defines several terms related to the subject, and article III determines that research involving human beings must comply with fundamental scientific and ethical requirements as defined in the Resolution while subsections 1, 2, and 3 of article III further define the ethical implications, standards, and requirements related to research involving human beings.

According to article IV, respect for human dignity requires that all research be conducted after informed consent from subjects, individuals, or groups by themselves and/or with the express agreement to participate in the research by their legal representatives. Article VII.1 requires that the institutions that perform research involving human beings must constitute, according to their needs, one or more Research Ethics Committees (*Comitê de Ética em Pesquisa*) and that all research involving human beings must be submitted to such committees.[26]

C. National Technical Commission on Biosafety

The CTNBio, which is part of the Ministry of Science and Technology, is a multidisciplinary collegial body with an advisory and deliberative character designed for the purpose of providing technical support and advice to the federal government in the preparation, updating, and implementation of the National Biosafety Policy of genetically modified organisms and their derivatives, as well as the establishment of technical standards of safety and technical advice regarding the authorization of activities involving research and the commercial use of genetically modified organisms and their derivatives based on the assessment of their risk (*risco zoofitossanitário*) to human health and the environment.[27]

The Technical Commission must monitor the development of, and technical and scientific progress in, the areas of biosafety, biotechnology, bioethics, and related areas, aiming to increase its capacity to protect human health, animals and plants, and the environment.[28] The CTNBio is composed of members and alternates appointed by the Minister of Science and Technology, and must have twenty-seven Brazilian citizens of recognized technical abilities and remarkable scientific knowledge and performance. The members must have an academic doctoral degree with professional activity in the areas of biosafety, biotechnology, biology, human and

---

[24] The National Council of Health is an agency subordinated to the Ministry of Health, composed of representatives of organizations and movements representing users, organizations representing health care workers, the government, and providers of health services. Its mission is to decide, supervise, and monitor public health policies. *Apresentação*, CONSELHO NACIONAL DE SAÚDE, http://conselho.saude.gov.br/apresentacao/apresentacao.htm (last visited Aug. 15, 2012).

[25] Resolução CNS No. 196, de ao de Outubro de 1996, RESOLUÇÕES, *Conselho Nacional de Saúde*, http://conselho.saude.gov.br/resolucoes/reso_96.htm.

[26] *Id.* art. VII.

[27] Lei No. 11.105, *supra* note 4, art. 10.

[28] *Id.* art. 10(sole para.)

animal health, or the environment as specified in article 11 of Law No. 11,105.[29] The functioning of the CTNBio is defined by the regulation of Law No. 11,105.[30]

D. National Biosafety Council

The CNBS is subordinated to the Presidency of the Republic and is a superior advisory body to the President for the preparation and implementation of the National Biosafety Policy.[31]

The Council is charged with the duty of establishing principles and guidelines for the administrative actions of federal agencies and entities with expertise on the subject;[32] analyzing applications for the commercial release of genetically modified organisms and their derivatives in matters regarding propriety, socioeconomic opportunity, and national interest, upon the request of the CTNBio;[33] and deciding, as the final hearing body, administrative cases relating to activities involving the commercial use of genetically modified organisms and their derivatives.[34]

Decree No. 5,591 further regulates the activities, functioning, and composition of CNBS, as well as the jurisdiction of the organs and entities in charge of registering, supervising, and authorizing proceedings related to genetically modified organisms and their derivatives.[35]

Although article 8 of Law No. 11, 105 charges the CNBS with the duty of preparing and implementing the National Biosafety Policy, it appears that such a policy has yet to be prepared and implemented.

E. National Bioethical Commission

On May 6, 2004, Federal Deputy Ivan Valente introduced a bill in the Chamber of Deputies that would create a National Commission on Bioethics (*Comissão Nacional de Bioética*) for the purpose of advising the government on ethical issues arising from health practices derived from scientific and technological advances in the fields of biology, medicine, and health that may pose a risk to human life and the environmental balance.[36] On October 10, 2005, the government sent a bill to the Chamber of Deputies proposing the creation of the National Bioethics Council (*Conselho Nacional de Bioética*).[37] As both bills were drafted for

---

[29] *Id.* art. 11.

[30] *Id.* art. 12. *See also* Decreto No. 5.591, *supra* note 5, art. 5 et seq.

[31] *Id.* art. 8.

[32] *Id.* art. 8(§1)(I).

[33] *Id.* art. 8(§1)(II).

[34] *Id.* art. 8(§1)(III).

[35] Decreto No. 5,591, *supra* note 5, arts. 48 et seq.

[36] Projeto de Lei No. 3.497/2004, Câmara dos Deputados, http://www.camara.gov.br/proposicoes Web/fichadetramitacao?idProposicao=252103&ord=1.

[37] Projeto de Lei No. 6.032/2005, Câmara dos Deputados, http://www.camara.gov.br/proposicoes Web/fichadetramitacao?idProposicao=302782.

the same purpose, they have been attached together and are waiting to be analyzed, debated, and voted on by the National Congress.

Prepared by Eduardo Soares
Senior Foreign Law Specialist
August 2012

LAW LIBRARY OF CONGRESS

RUSSIAN FEDERATION

REGULATION OF ACTIVITIES RELATING TO BIOTECHNOLOGY

Executive Summary

While human dignity is protected under the Constitution, Russian legislation does not directly address ethical issues and does not define scientific ethics and bioethics. Ethical norms are regulated by professional organizations of scientists. Patent and copyright infringement appears to be the only prosecutable offense in the field of science. Human cloning is prohibited and genetic modification is under government control. Russia is not a party to the European Bioethics Convention, and a competent public authority in charge of adopting ethics-related decisions has not been established, although there are several federal entities with consultative functions.

I. General Overview

Russian legislation does not define such terms as "scientific ethics" or "bioethics." In 1997, the government drafted the Bill on Legal Foundations of Biomedical Ethics and Guarantees of Its Implementation, but it was not approved by the legislature.[1] Ethical requirements for scientific work are discussed primarily by scholars and academics and are regulated by professional organizations. For example, the Union of Scientific and Engineering Organizations issued the Ethics Code of Scientists and Engineers in 2002, which focuses on the following ethical aspects of scientific work:

- the necessity of keeping a high level of competency among scientists,

- respect for fellow scientists and avoidance of intellectual rights infringement, and

- demonstrating respect in the application of scientific results to human beings.[2]

In 2010, four roundtables on biological and medical ethics were conducted by the Russian Academy of Sciences. While discussing connections between medical technological

---

[1] *See* Olga Starovoitova, *Regulirovanie Poriadka Provedeniia Meditsinskogo Eksperimenta* [*Procedures for Conducting a Medical Experiment*], MEDITSINSKOE PRAVO, 2005, No. 1, *available at* http://www.lawmix. ru/med/3196.

[2] Ethics Code of Scientists and Engineers, Russian Union of Scientific and Engineering Organizations, 2002, *available at* http://rusea.info/tree/?id=15.

achievements and bioethics, the participants confirmed a conclusion that bioethics must protect the rights of the individual (patient) and be based on fundamental human rights.[3]

To some extent, the ethical aspects of scientists' competence are regulated by the Russian Academy of Science; however, this fact causes concern among scientists, who believe that such an approach slows down the evolution of new ideas. No other aspect of scholarly ethics seems to be covered by the Russian Academy of Science.[4]

With regard to international cooperation in the field of bioethics, Russia joined the International Center for Genetic Engineering and Biotechnology in 1992,[5] participates in the UNESCO Intergovernmental Bioethics Commission (IGBC),[6] and has a representative at the Council of Europe Steering Committee on Bioethics (CDBI).[7] Russia did not sign the Council of Europe Convention for the Protection of Human Rights and Dignity of the Human Being with regard to the Application of Biology and Medicine. The absence of a competent body in charge of adopting decisions on bioethics issues was named as the main reason for not joining the Convention.[8]

II. Legal Framework

The major legal principle related to bioethics is included in article 21 of the Russian Constitution, which states that "[h]uman dignity shall be protected by the State. Nobody shall be subject to medical, scientific, or other experiments without his/her voluntary consent."[9]

Russian Federal Law on Science and Scientific and Technical Policies[10] does not address issues of ethics directly. However, some ethical provisions can be derived from that Law. Article 4(6) of the Law states that a scientist can refuse to participate in research, which

---

[3] *Scientists Discussed the Problem of Organ Transplantation and Other Issues of Bioethics*, RUSSIAN ACADEMY OF SCIENCES (Apr. 23, 2010), http://ras.ru/news/shownews.aspx?id=52cd3cf6-cc58-494c-9d57-3c49fc650798#content (in Russian).

[4] V. Zhigalov, *Nuzhna Li Nauke Etika?* [*Does Science Need Ethics?*], *available at* http://www.chronos.msu ru/discussions/zhigalov_ethics.pdf (in Russian; last visited Aug. 10, 2012).

[5] Government Resolution No. 765, Oct. 7, 1992, *available at* http://pravo.gov ru/proxy/ips/?doc body=&nd=102018535&intelsearch=%E3%E5%ED%ED%E0%FF+%E8%ED%E6%E5%ED%E5%F0%E8%FF (in Russian; official publication).

[6] *IGBC*, UNESCO,http://www.unesco.org/new/en/social-and-human-sciences/themes/bioethics/intergovernmental-bioethics-committee/ (last visited Aug. 7, 2012).

[7] *Council of Europe, Secretariat Memorandum, Steering Committee on Bioethics, Information Document Concerning the CDBI* (Oct. 5, 2011), http://www.coe.int/t/dg3/healthbioethic/cdbi/INF_2011_%201REV%20E%20 info%20doc%20cdbi.pdf.

[8] Boris Iudin, *Prava Cheloveka I Biomeditsina* [*Human Rights and Biomedicine*] para. 14, *available at* http://md-sgi narod ru/doc2_2.html (in Russian).

[9] KONSTITUTSIIA ROSSIISKOI FEDERATSII [CONSTITUTION] art. 21, http://pravo.gov.ru/export/sites/default/konstituciya/Konst_2011.pdf (official publication; last visited Aug. 10, 2012).

[10] SOBRANIE ZAKONODTELSTVA ROSSIISKOI FEDEREATSII [SZ RF] [COLLECTION OF RUSSIAN LEGISLATION] (official gazette) 1996, No. 35, Item 4137.

negatively affects a human, society, and the environment. Article 4(7) establishes that a scientist's duty is to conduct scientific, technical, and experimental works in a way that does not violate human rights and freedom, and does not harm one's health and the environment. When this bill was discussed in the legislature, it contained a provision (art. 5) that required scientists to be governed by the norms of scientific ethics and bear moral responsibility for economic, environmental, and other socially significant results of their work. For unknown reasons, this provision was not included in the final version of the Law.[11]

Indirectly, specific ethics issues are addressed in legal acts regulating the testing of medicine, human cloning, and genetic engineering.

A. Medical and Pharmaceutical Research

The 2010 Federal Law on Circulation of Medicines[12] contains a number of provisions relating to ethical issues in medicine testing. In order to get permission to conduct testing, which is a precondition for a medicine's registration, the manufacturing company must undergo an evaluation to confirm the ethical character of the testing (art. 17). This ethical evaluation is conducted by the Ethics Council, which was established under the Federal Ministry of Healthcare and Social Protection on August 31, 2010.[13] The Council includes representatives of scientific and educational institutions, nongovernmental research organizations, religious organizations, and mass media. Legal documents regulating the work of the Ethics Council do not define what makes medicine testing appropriate from the ethical point of view, and all decisions appear to be made on a case-by-case basis. The Statute on the Council states that its activities must be conducted according to principles of legality, conformity with human rights, experts' independence, and impartiality. Inconclusive research results cannot be brought for the Council's evaluation.[14]

B. Human Genetic Technology

The conduct of genetic engineering and the application of genetic treatment to the human body, tissues, or cells are not covered by the Federal Law on State Regulation in the Field of Genetic Engineering Activities,[15] the major legal act in the field, which introduced state regulation of all activities related to genetic technologies and requires their mandatory licensing. According to amendments to this law dated June 28, 2000, all "genetic manipulations on the molecular and cellular levels for the purposes of genetic diagnostics and/or genetic therapy in

---

[11] Resolution of the Federation Council (upper chamber) of the Russian Federation Federal Assembly (legislature), No. 157 of July 12, 1994, http://pravo.gov.ru/proxy/ips/?docbody=&nd=102030974&intelsearch= %EE+%EF%F0%EE%E5%EA%F2%E5+%F4%E5%E4%E5%F0%E0%EB%FC%ED%EE%E3%EE+%E7%E0% EA%EE%ED%E0+%CE+%ED%E0%F3%EA%E5+%E8+%ED%E0%F3%F7%ED%EE- %F2%E5%F5%ED%E8%F7%E5%F1%EA%EE%E9 (official publication).

[12] SZ RF 2010, No. 16, Item 1815.

[13] ROSSIISKAIA GAZETA (official publication) Sept. 17, 2010, http://www.rg.ru/2010/09/17/sovet-dok.html.

[14] *Id.*

[15] SZ RF 1996, No. 28, Item 3348.

regard to the human" must be licensed by federal authorities.[16] The law states that products and services made by genetic engineering methods must meet the requirements of environmental safety, sanitation, and pharmaceutical norms, and the federal standards of the Russian Federation.

On April 19, 2002, the Parliament of Russia adopted the Federal Law on the Temporary Ban on Human Cloning.[17] The Law imposed a moratorium on human cloning and prohibited the transportation of cloned human embryos across the country's border. Russian legislators stated that this action was based on respect for the dignity of a human beings, the recognition of a human's value, the necessity of protecting personal rights and freedoms, and insufficient knowledge of the potential biological and social consequences of human cloning. The Law reserved the opportunity to extend the ban or waive it as necessary knowledge is accumulated, and as appropriate moral, social, and ethical norms are identified. In 2010, the Law was amended to ban cloning for an indefinite period of time.[18] The waiver of the cloning ban was conditioned on the adoption of a law on procedures for cloning,[19] which has not yet been passed.

In compliance with this provision, paragraph 4 of article 1349 of the Russian Civil Code provides that methods of human cloning cannot be patented. Together with human cloning methods, the same paragraph bans patenting the methods and techniques for the genetic modification of human embryo cells, the use of human embryos for industrial purposes, and other activities conflicting with social concerns and principles of humanity and morality.[20]

The moratorium on human cloning does not apply to the cloning of other organisms. The ban does not prohibit research into therapeutic cloning or the cloning of animals and individual organs of the human body.[21] Clinical microbiological laboratories, which are allowed to conduct research on cloning, and clinics that conduct cell research are subject to government control.[22] In 2003, the Ministry of Healthcare and Social Protection designated sixteen research centers where cloning experiments are allowed.[23]

---

[16] SZ RF 2000, No. 29, Item 3005.

[17] SZ RF 2002, No. 21, Item 1917.

[18] SZ RF 2010, No. 14, Item 1550.

[19] *Id.* art. 1.

[20] SZ RF 2006, No. 52(1), Item 5496.

[21] Interview with Health Care and Social Protection Minister T. Golikova, Rossiia Prodlit Moratorii na Klonirovanie Cheloveka [Russia Will Extend Human Cloning Moratorium] (Oct. 2, 2009), *available at* http://medportal.ru/mednovosti/news/2009/10/02/clones/ (in Russian, last visited Aug. 10, 2012).

[22] SZ RF 1998, No. 3, Item 211.

[23] Order of the Russian Federation Ministry of Healthcare and Social Protection No. 333 of August 5, 2003 on the Development of the Medical Genetic Services, *available at* http://base.consultant.ru/cons/cgi/online.cgi?req=doc;base=EXP;n=333775 (in Russian).

C. Genetic Engineering

Legislation on genetically modified medicines, food, and food products addresses some ethical issues by ordering the disclosure of information on genetic engineering-related activity (art. 10) and the mandatory certification and standardization of genetically modified (GM) products (art. 11).[24]

Policies are set and monitored by the Interagency Commission for Problems of Genetic Engineering Activity, which includes representatives from different executive agencies, academia, biological research institutions, medical circles, and military services, and was established under the Prime Minister of Russia. All GM food products, GM raw materials, and GM food additives manufactured, distributed, or sold over the counter in Russia must be registered with the National Register of Genetically Modified Food Products. The registration is valid for three years and may be extended for an additional five years.[25] All food products received from GM sources must pass federally established testing in order to determine whether a genetically altered new organism poses any danger in comparison to the original.[26] Special labeling is required for GM products, products based on GM sources, and products containing components received from GM sources.[27] Foreign economic operations with genetically modified microorganisms (GMMs) are also subject to government control, and the list of GMMs allowed for export from Russia must be approved by the Russian Federation President.[28]

III. Regulatory Institutions

Russia has not established a competent public authority to address issues relating to bioethics and to be in charge of adopting ethics-related decisions. It appears that there are six different federal bodies dealing with bioethics. They include national committees on bioethics at the Russian Academy of Science, Russian Academy of Medical Science, Russian Medical Society, and Association of Physicians; the Ethics Council under the Ministry of Healthcare and Social Protection;[29] and the national Bioethics Committee under the Russian Commission on UNESCO Affairs.[30] All of these organizations have consultative functions and are not entitled to adopt mandatory decisions.

---

[24] SZ RF 1996, No. 28, Item 3348.

[25] GENNAIA INZHENERIIA: SBORNIK PRAVOVYH DOKUMENTOV [GENETIC ENGINEERING: COLLECTION OF LEGAL ACTS] 93–94 (Moscow, Ministry of Health Protection, 2001).

[26] SZ RF 2000, No. 51, Item 4996.

[27] Ministry of Health Protection Resolution, No. 12 of September 12, 1999, *in* ZASCHITA PRAV POTREBITELIA [CONSUMER PROTECTION] 37 (Moscow, Yurait, 2001).

[28] Government Regulation No. 634 of August 29, 2001, SZ RF 2001, No. 34, Item 3751.

[29] MIKHAIL LOPUKHIN, BIOETIKA: IZBRANNYE STATYI I DOKLADY [BIOETHICS: SELECTED ARTICLES AND REPORTS] 16 (Moscow, 2003) (in Russian).

[30] *Russian Bioethics Committee Has Been Established*, RUSSIAN ACADEMY OF SCIENCES (Dec. 20, 2006), http://ras.ru/news/shownews.aspx?id=c34b8cd5-3a88-4b39-bb8d-0e5b0a4debe2#content (in Russian; last visited Aug. 8, 2012).

As mentioned above, there are two additional government commissions in the field of medicine testing and genetic engineering. They coordinate activities of different agencies and provide suggestions regarding the formulation and implementation of state policies in related fields.

IV. Enforcement

With regard to scientific activities, relevant Criminal Code provisions can be found in articles 146 and 147, which penalize the infringement of patent rights and copyright. Even though human cloning is prohibited, the law is silent concerning the punishment for violating the cloning ban rules. A provision addressing the failure to conduct an ethical evaluation during the testing of medicines also could not be located. It appears that license revocation is the only form of punishment foreseen for the distribution of medicines that are not properly registered.

In 1994, the Supreme Court of the Russian Federation addressed the issue of bioethics in Ruling No. 3 of April 28, 1994, on Judicial Practice in Regard to Health Damage Compensation Cases. Because of the existing inability to exercise total control over human genetic technologies, the Court recognized all works in this field as activities that cause an increased danger to human health.[31] This ruling appears to be the only decision to date that reflects a judicial perspective on human genetic technologies.

Prepared by Peter Roudik,
Director of Legal Research,
and Virab Khachatryan,
Interning Foreign Law Specialist
August 2012

---

[31] BULLETEN' VERKHOVNOGO SUDA ROSSIISKOI FEDERATSII [RUSSIAN FEDERATION SUPREME COURT BULLETIN] 1994, No. 6, at 12.

www.ingramcontent.com/pod-product-compliance
Lightning Source LLC
Chambersburg PA
CBHW080723190526
45169CB00006B/2499